Backyard Birds of the Piedmont

Flying through the sky or sitting in trees,
birds are all around us ...
singing songs that make us happy.

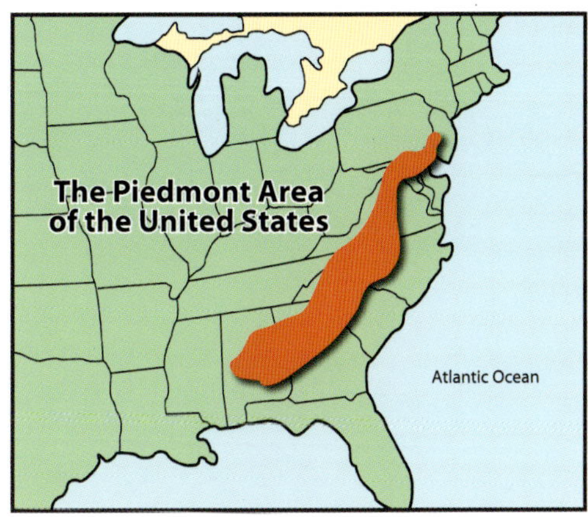

Written by
Suzanne Walls

Photography by
D. W. Maiden

Published in the United States by Chantilly Books, a division of Bonne Amie Publishing.

Cover photograph, "Red-headed Woodpecker"; by D. W. Maiden.

ISBN 978-0-9841960-8-1

Printed in China.

To Lauren and Tal,

With Love

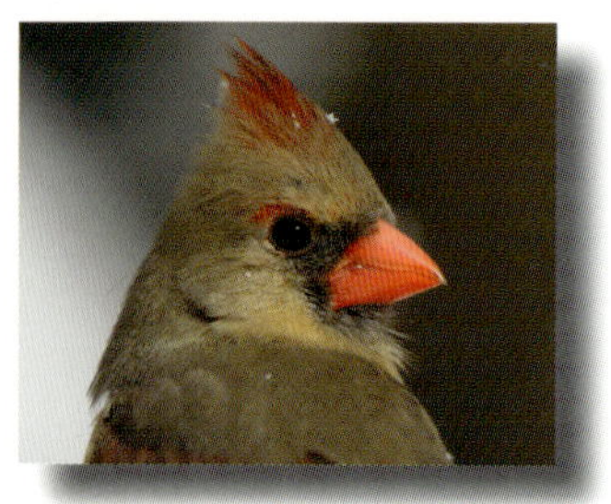

Northern Cardinal

We are Northern Cardinals and we love to sing! When we build nests and lay eggs, the mother sings a song telling the daddy when to bring food. People used to try to catch us because of our beautiful, red feathers. They took us up north ... even to Europe! Then, a law was passed to keep us safe. Today, there are lots of us around and we are happy!

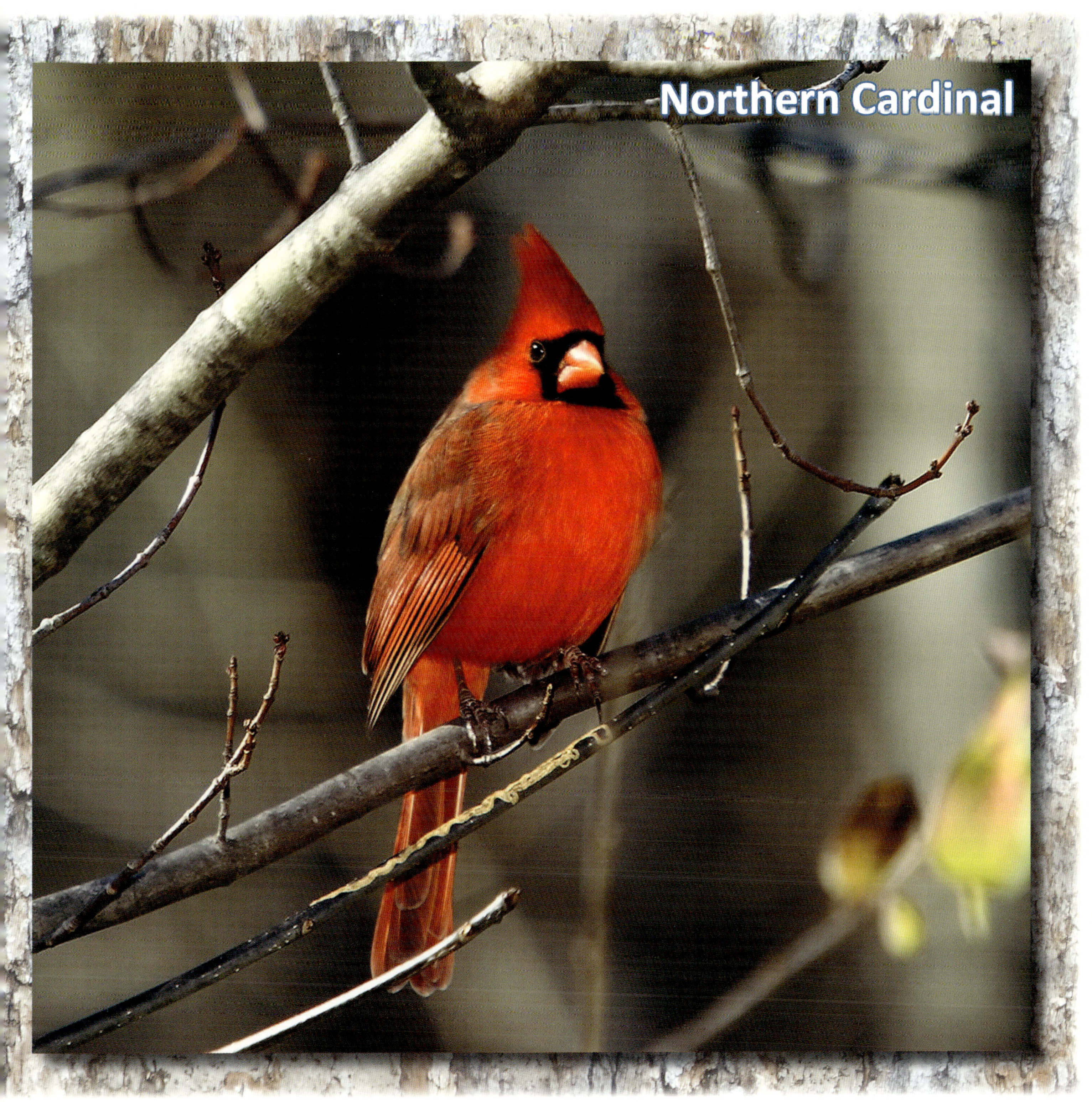
Northern Cardinal

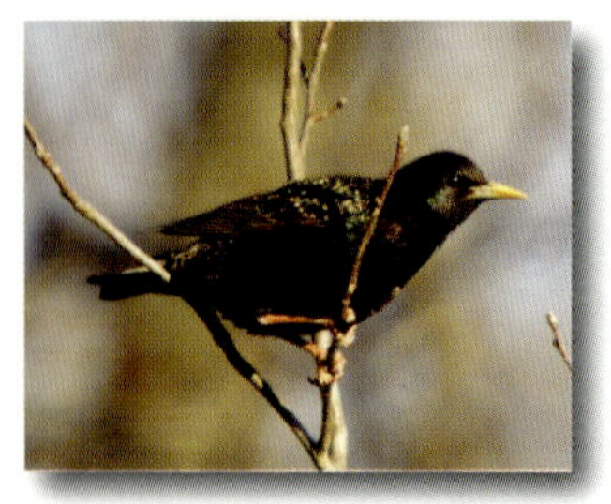

European Starling

Hi, I'm a European Starling. A long time ago,

people brought less than 100 of us to

the United States from Europe.

They set us free in Central Park in New York City!

Today, there are more than 200 million of us ...

that's a lot of birds!

We really like it here; but, we kill other birds.

Now people try to make us go away.

I must be very careful I don't get caught!

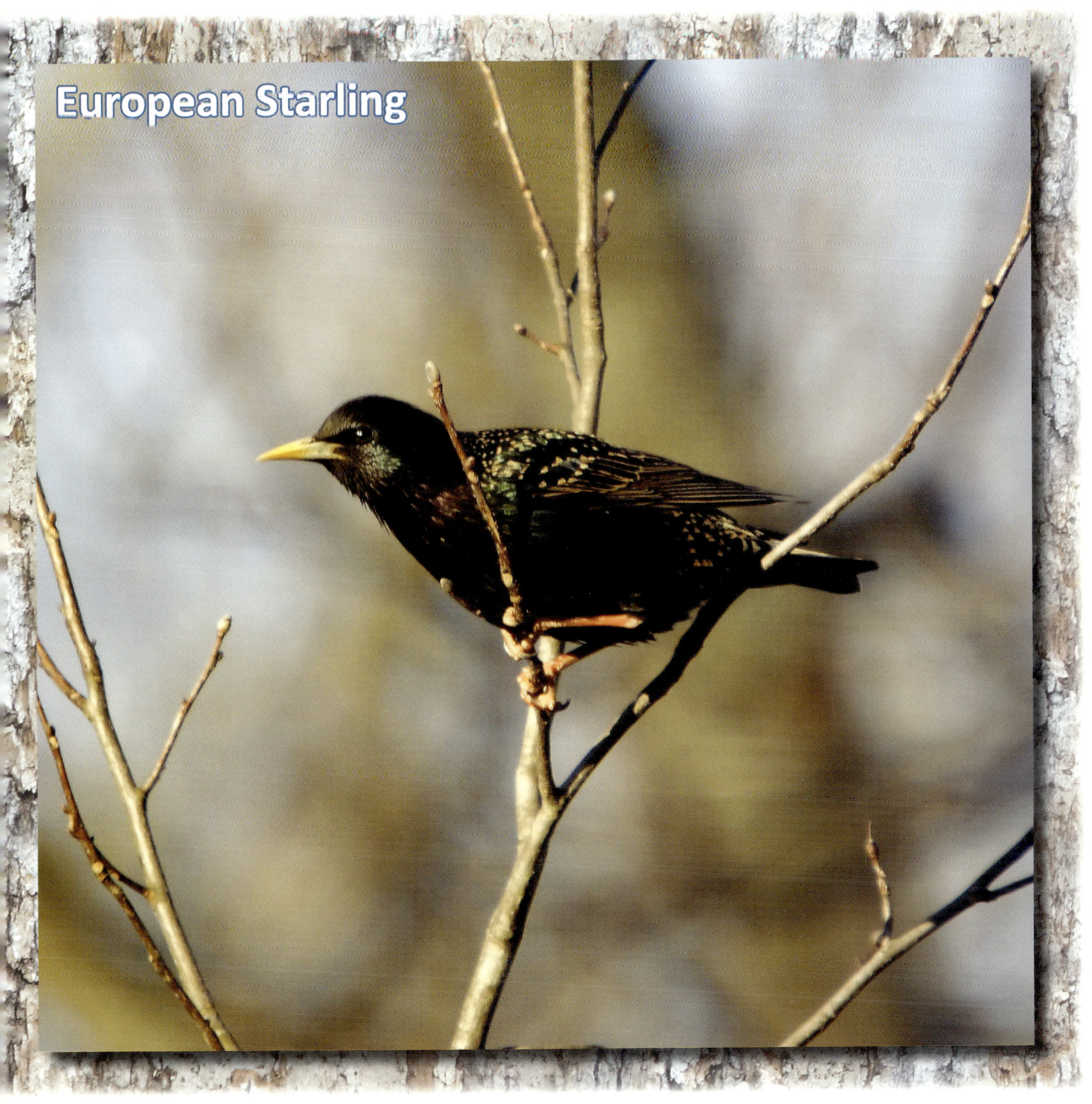
European Starling

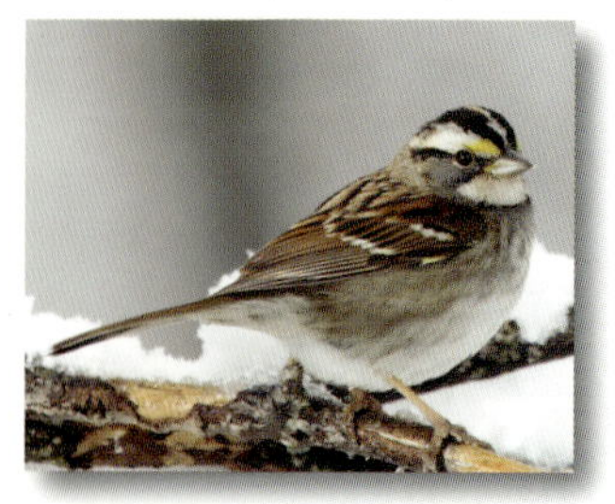

White-throated Sparrow

There are many different types of Sparrows. I'm called a White-throated Sparrow because of the white feathers under my chin. I also have black and tan stripes on top of my head. I use my feet to scratch the ground to find seeds buried in the dirt below where other birds eat. The seeds may not be clean, but they sure are tasty!

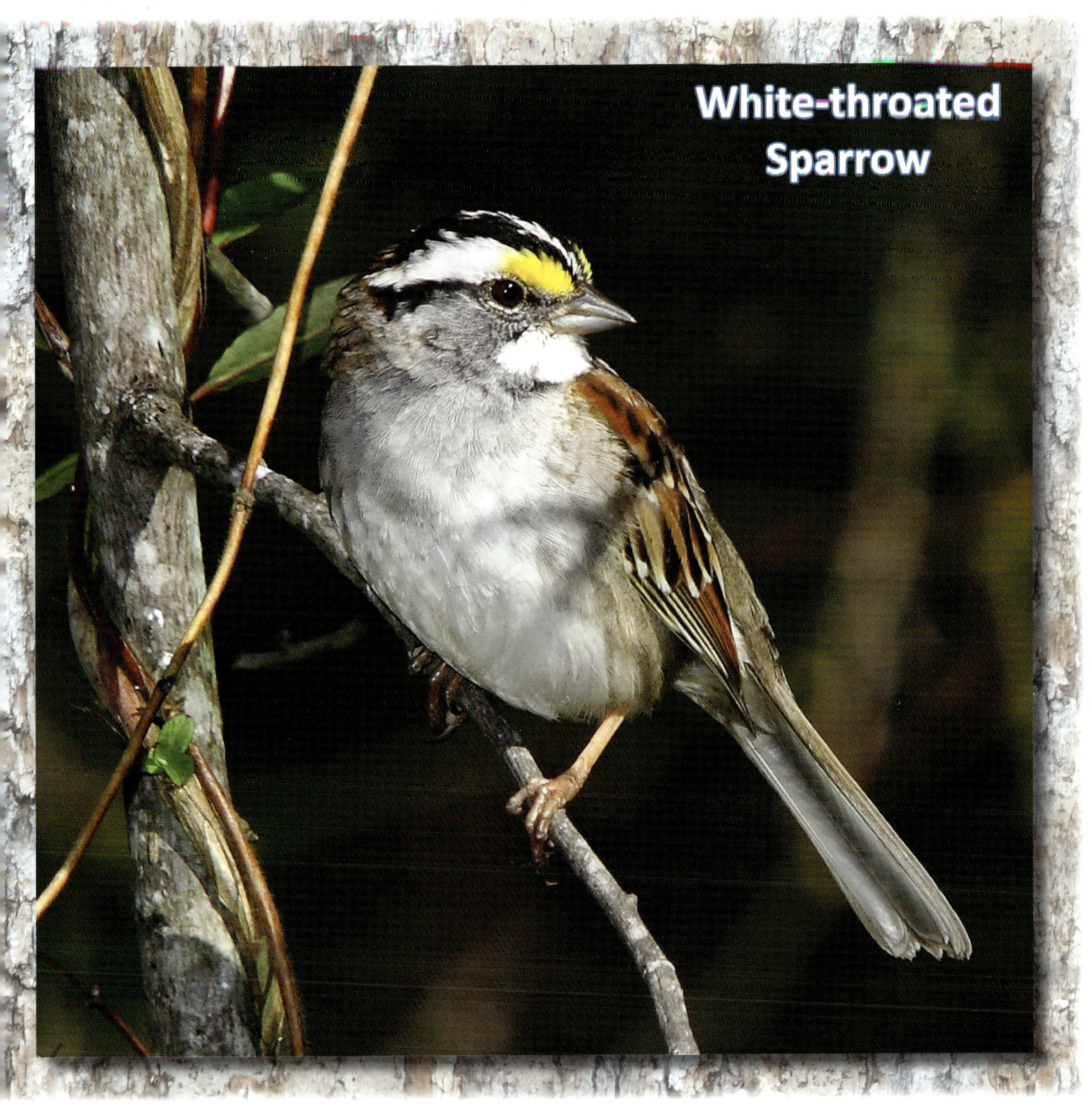
White-throated
Sparrow

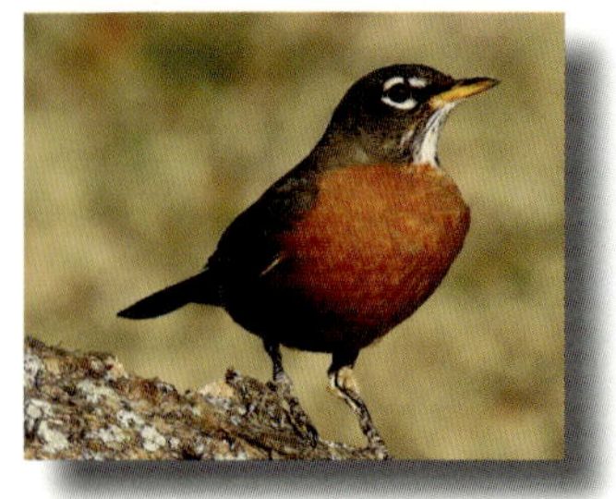

American Robin

Have you seen any worms around here?

Robins like big, juicy worms for dinner.

Sometimes we like to eat fruit too.

When it's cold outside, we huddle together

in large flocks. We hide in the woods until spring.

Then we come out from hiding.

People say we are a sure sign that spring is near.

After a long, cold winter

everyone is very happy to see us!

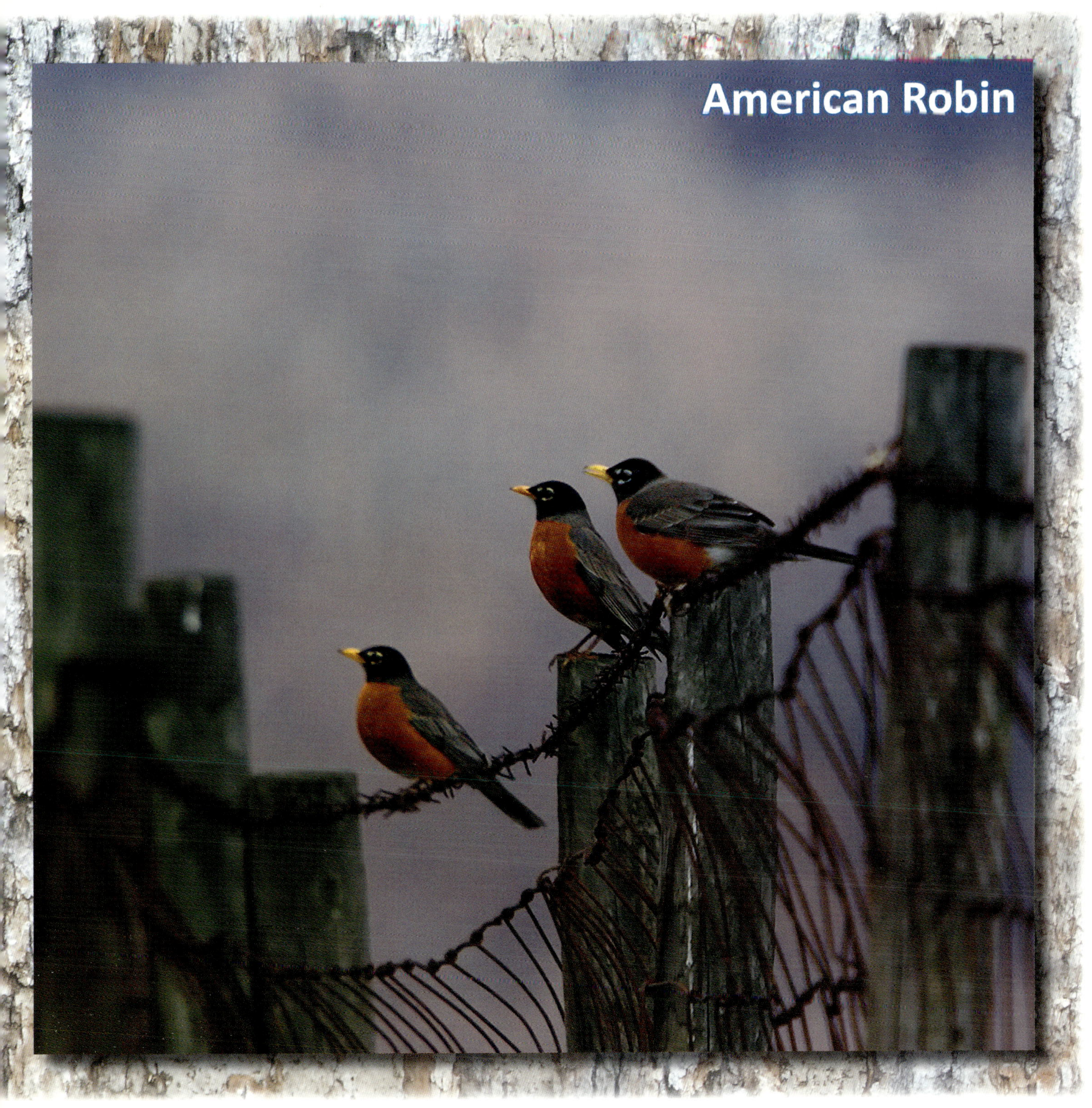
American Robin

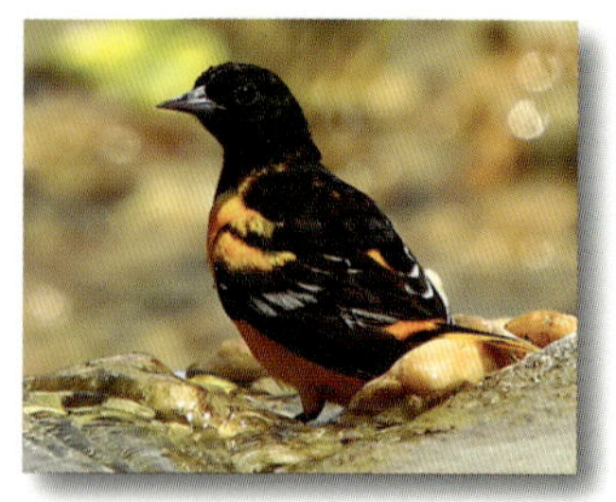

Baltimore Oriole

Maybe you have seen me in your yard. I am a Baltimore Oriole, and I like to build nests in shade trees. During the winter, I fly to South America where it's warm. Then, I return to the Piedmont in the springtime. My nest looks like a bag made of twigs and small branches … like a sleeping bag for birds. Maybe we can have a sleepover!

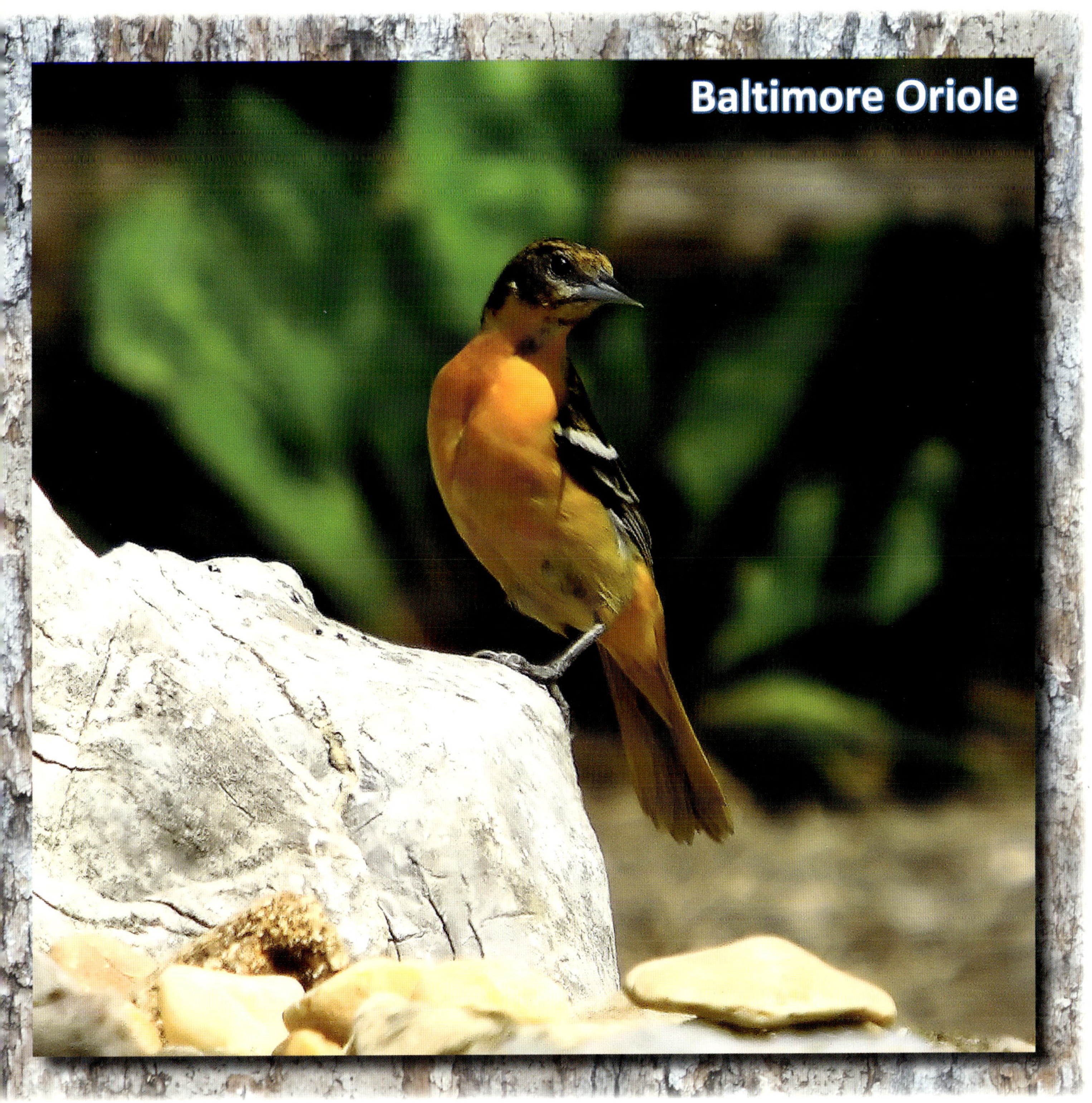
Baltimore Oriole

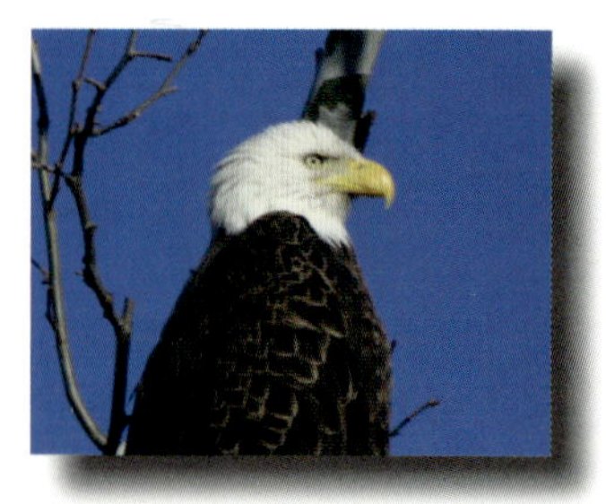

Bald Eagle

Do you know me? I'm a bald eagle.

Way back in 1782, I was selected to be

the symbol of the United States.

Eagles like me have excellent eyesight.

We are good swimmers and fishers, too.

Once there were only a few eagles,

so they put us on the Endangered Species List.

Now there are many more of us living in the wild.

Thank you for helping us survive!

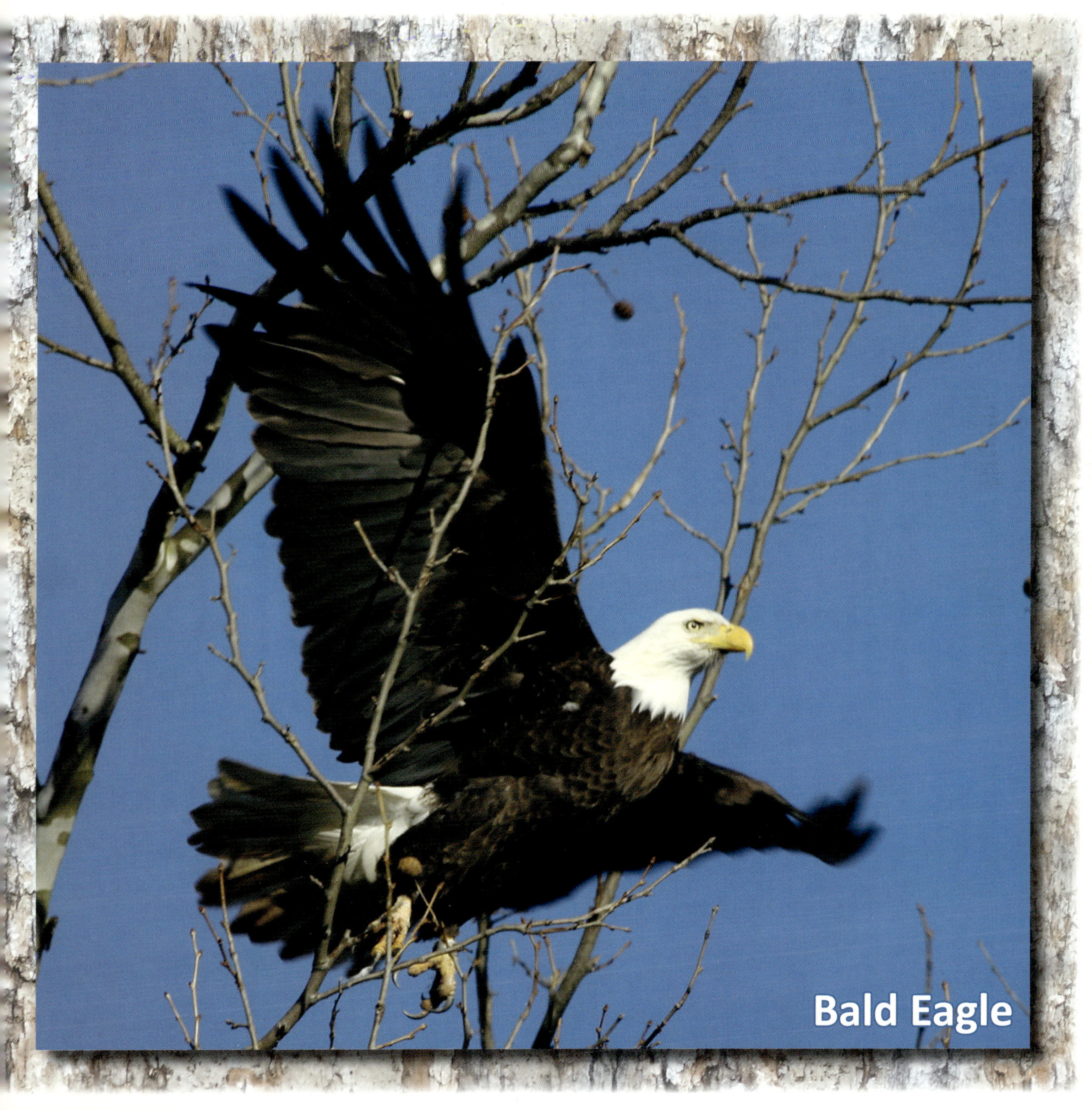

Bald Eagle

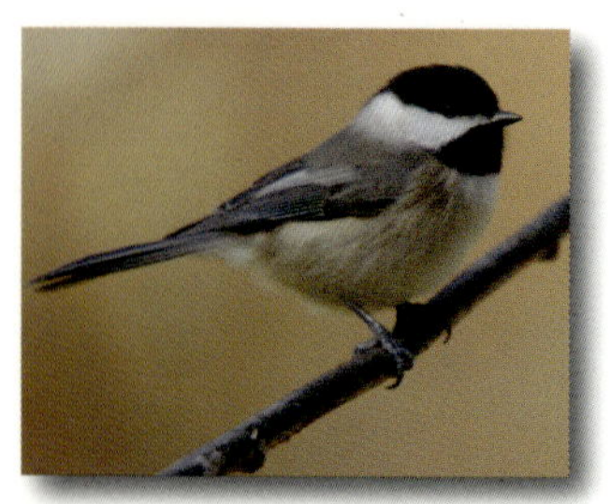

Black-capped Chickadee

Hi, I'm a Chickadee and I'm very friendly. If you put some seed in your hand and sit still for a while, I might even sit on your palm. When I find a seed, I hide it. Even though I might hide seeds in many different places, I can still find it a month later! Do you think my memory is better than an elephant's? Maybe ...!

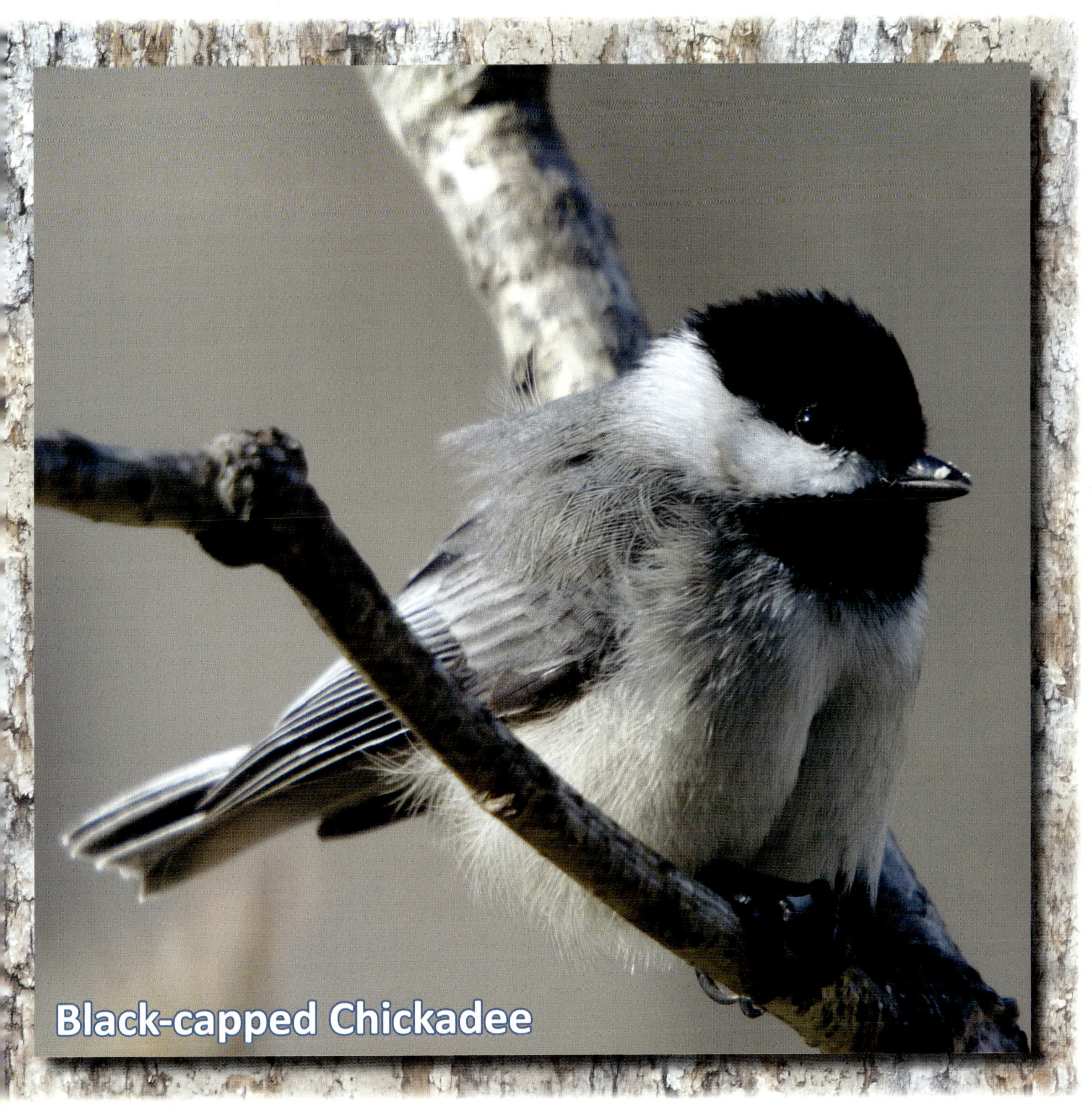

Black-capped Chickadee

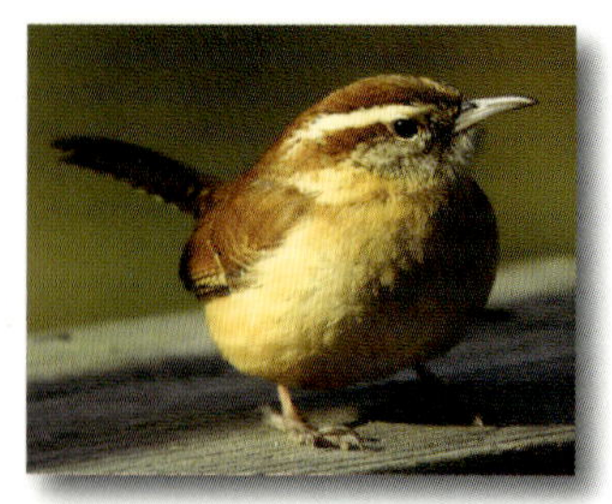

Carolina Wren

Hold your ears! I'm a Carolina Wren,

and I sing many different songs.

If I'm afraid, I sing very loud and try to

sound mean to tell other birds or animals

"Leave me alone!"

Sometimes I sing along with other

Wrens to make beautiful music.

If you build a birdhouse, I will make

my nest there and sing you a song!

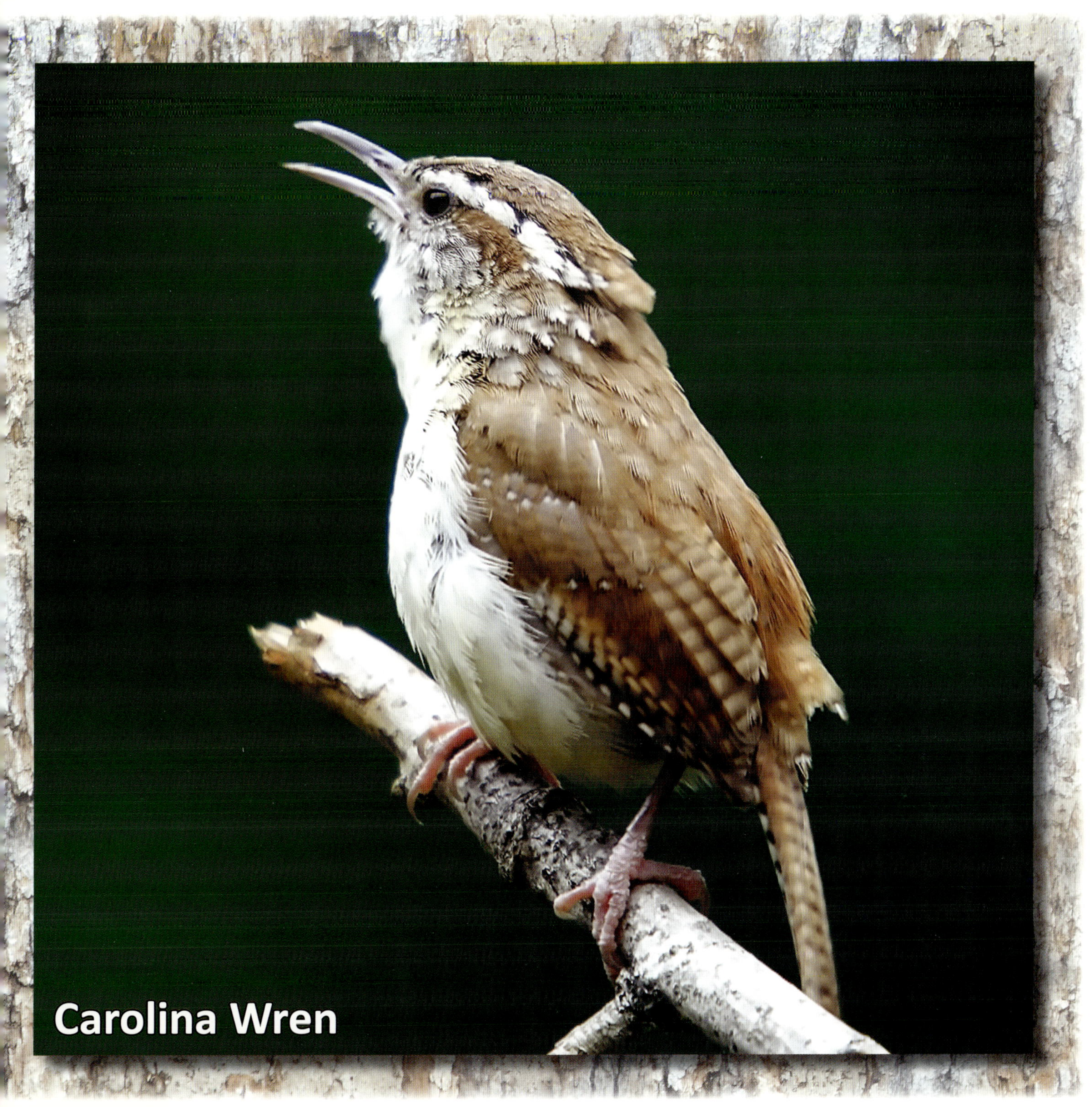

Carolina Wren

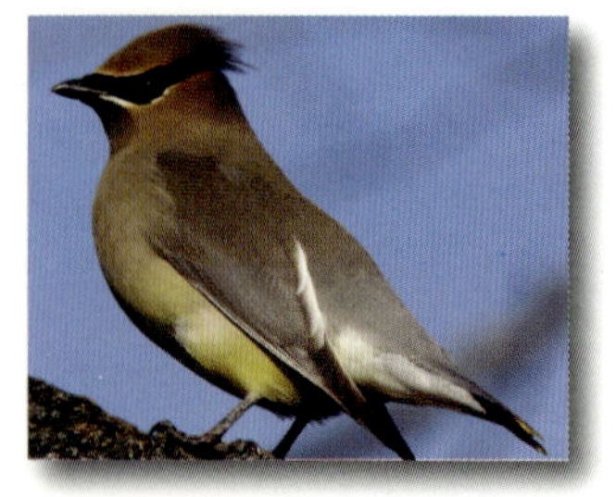

Cedar Waxwing

Have you ever seen a Cedar tree?

A lot of them grow in the Piedmont area.

I love to eat the small cones they grow on their branches. People named me after those trees. They call me a Cedar Waxwing. Besides cedar cones, I eat berries and fruit too. Sometimes my friends and I line up along a twig and pass berries down to each bird so everyone can eat.

We like to take care of each other!

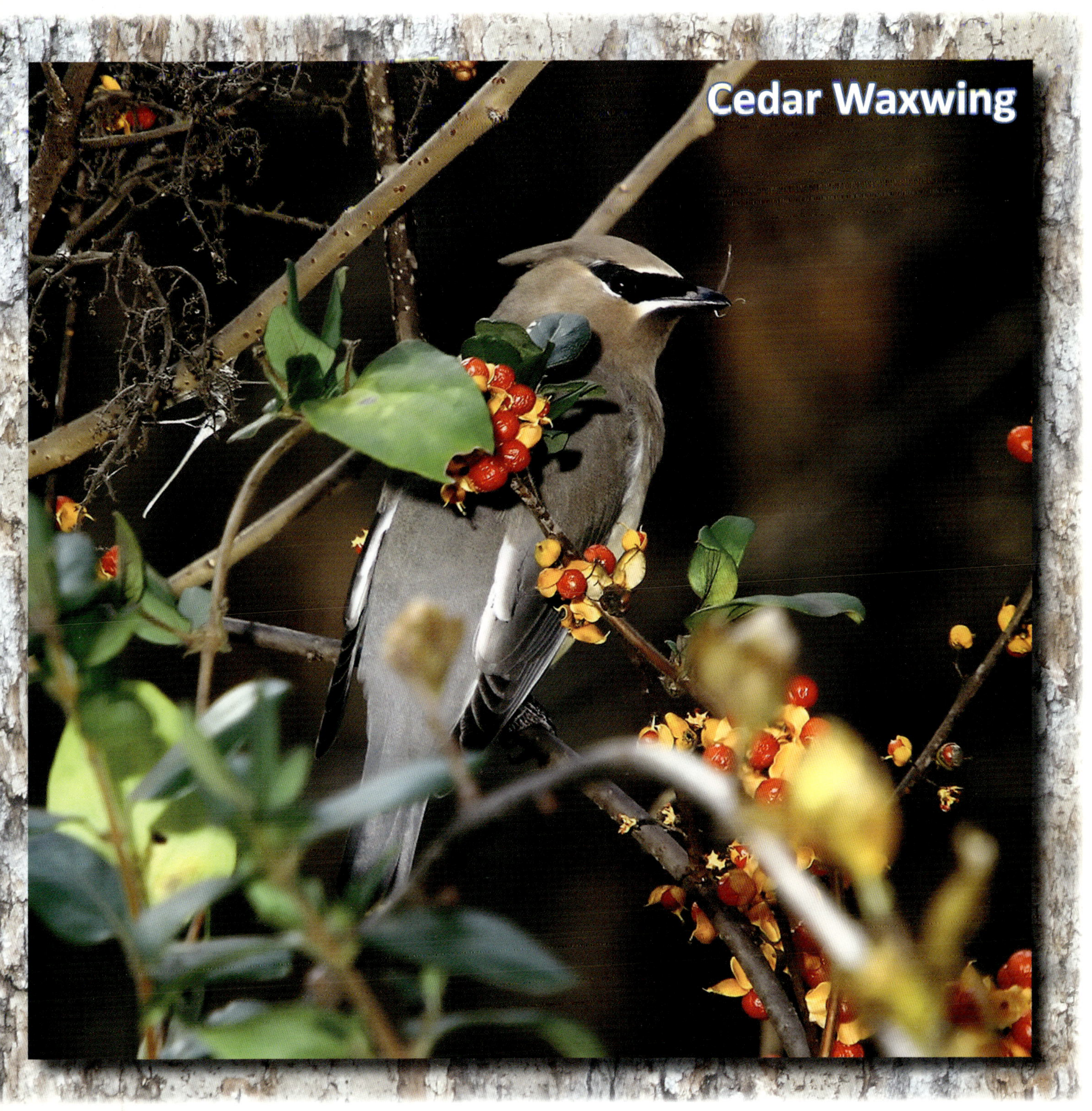
Cedar Waxwing

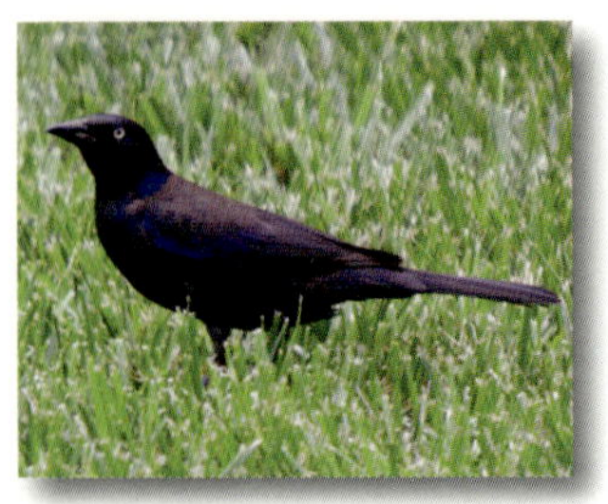

Common Grackle

My name may not be very pretty,

but my feathers are beautiful.

See the purple and blue colors

in my glossy black feathers?

I'm always looking for food, including seeds and grains. But I like to eat insects and mice.

I like to catch small fish, too.

Would you like to go fishing with me?

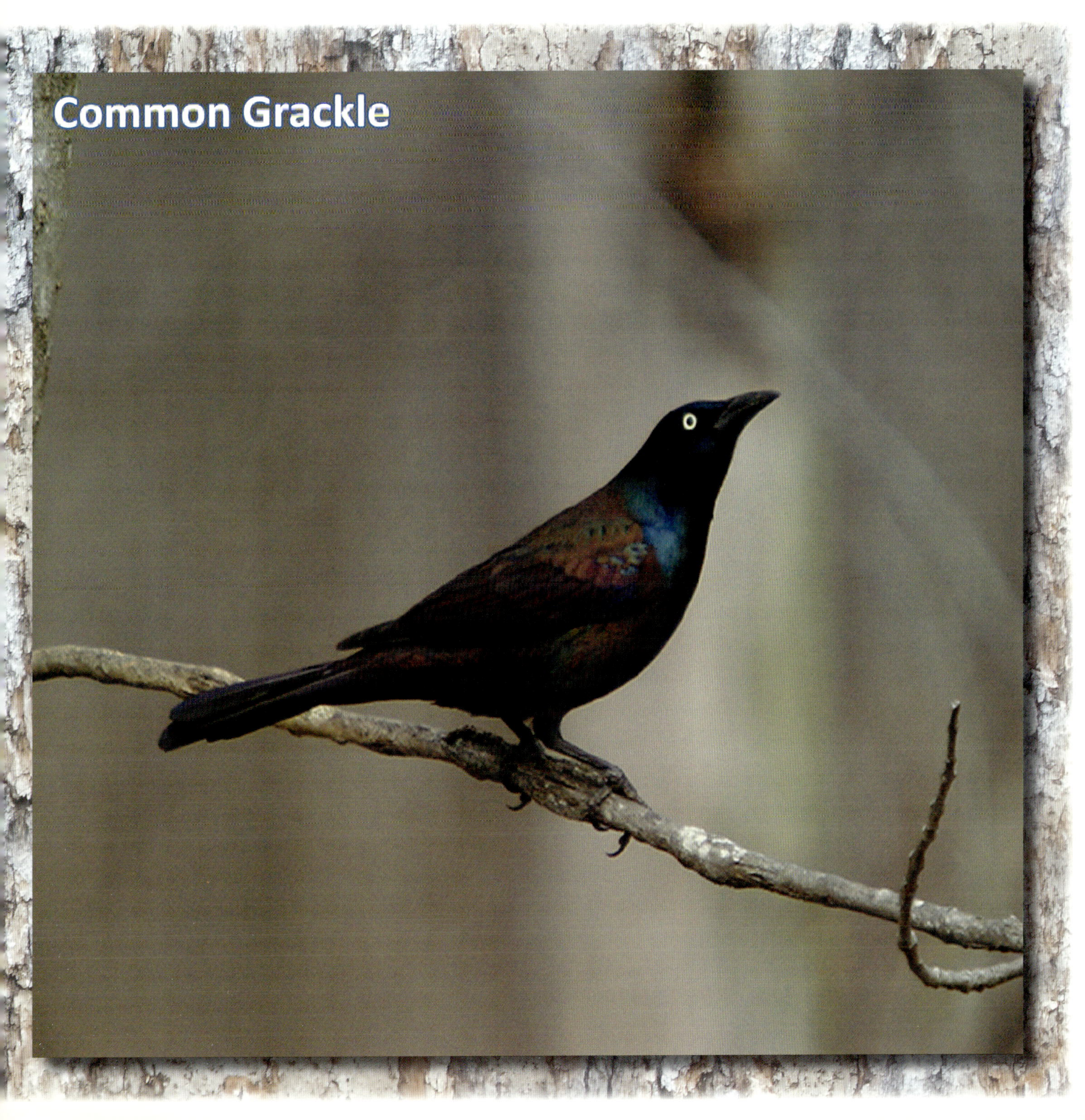
Common Grackle

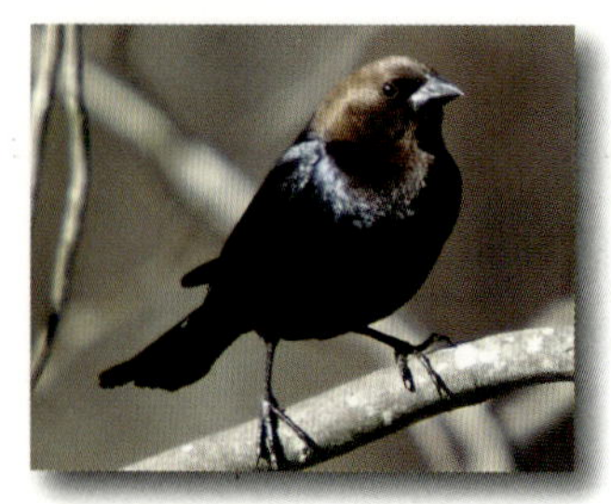

Cowbird

Cowbirds are the smallest of all the Blackbirds. Back in the 1800s, we lived in the western part of the United States where we followed Buffalo herds. Instead of building our own nests, we prefer to steal the nests of other birds. When male Cowbirds like us want to show off, we puff up our feathers so we look bigger! Do I look bigger to you?

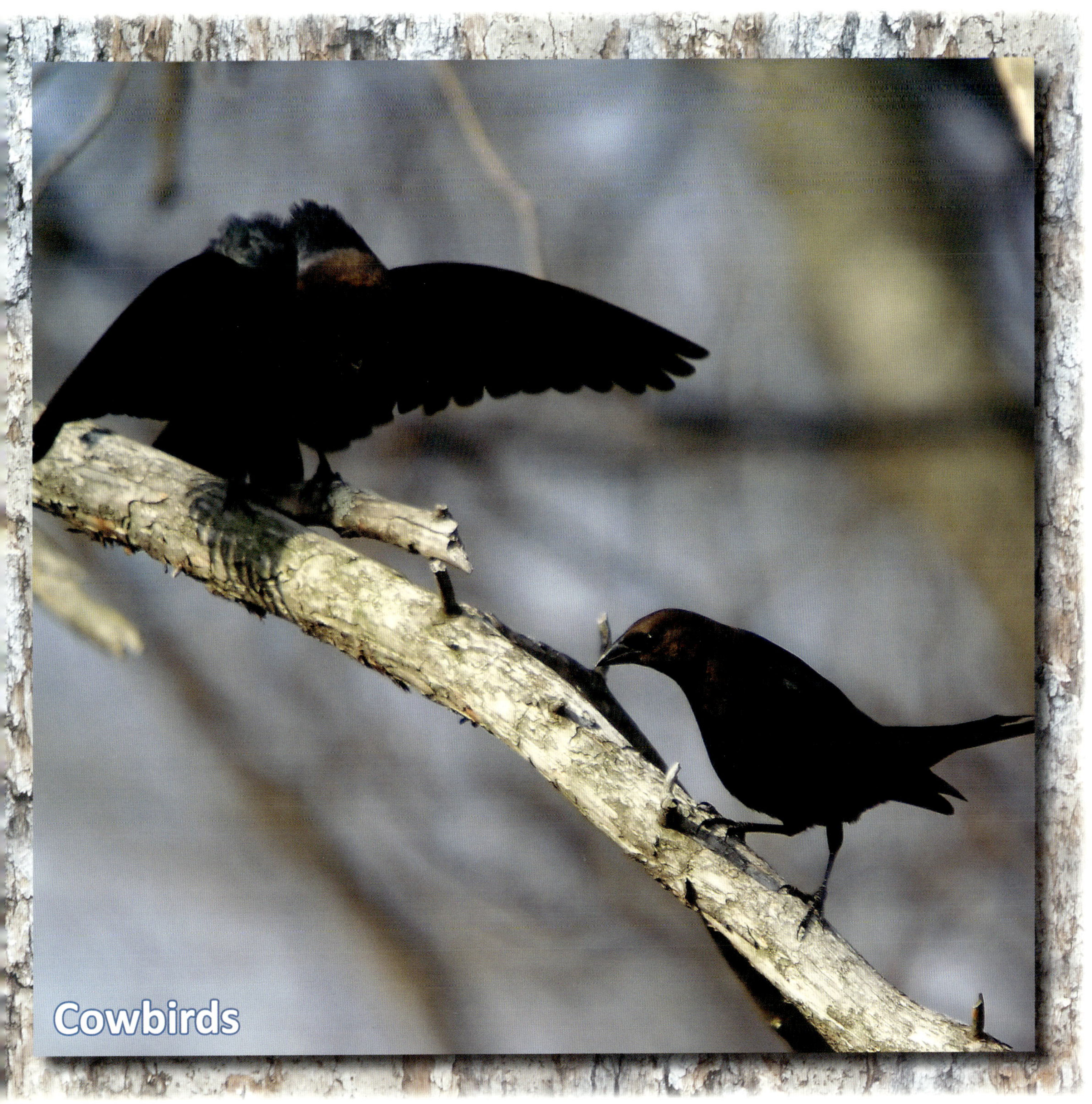
Cowbirds

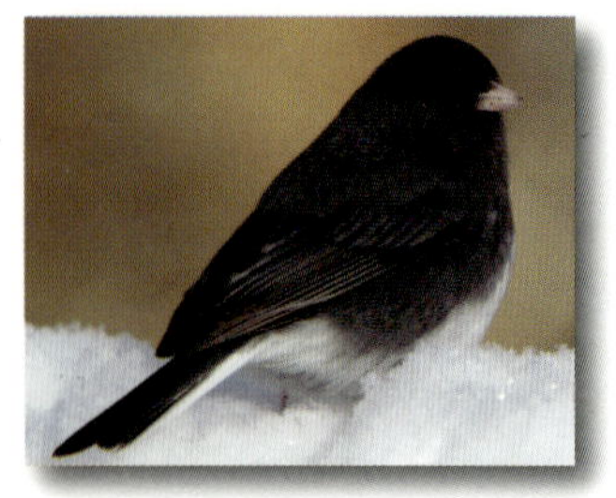

Dark-eyed Junco

Dark-eyed Juncos are cousins of White-throated Sparrows. You can tell I'm a Junco because of my plain body and dark head. When the weather gets cold, I fly toward warmer weather. If there's enough food around, I sometimes stay in the Piedmont area. Juncos are "ground feeders" ... we eat the seeds other birds drop. We're the cleanup crew in the backyard.

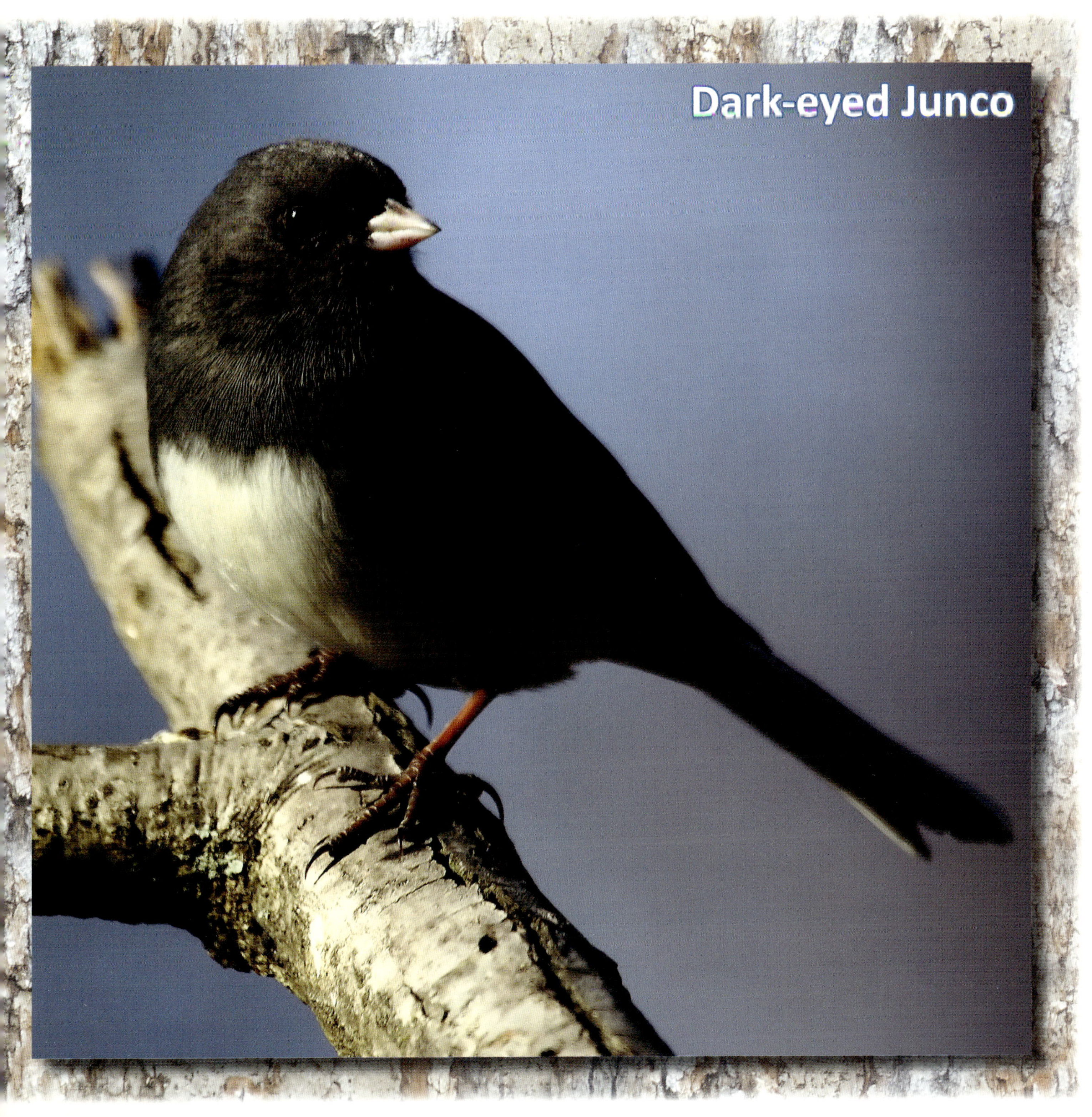
Dark-eyed Junco

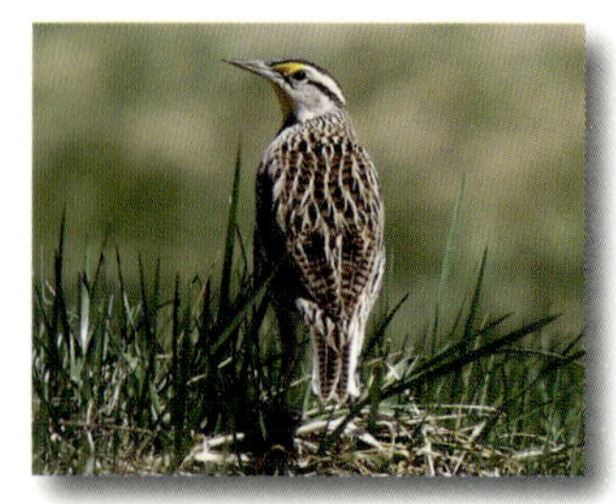

Eastern Meadowlark

Do you hear me singing? Meadowlarks sing a beautiful song. I live in hay fields and other grassy areas where I find my food. Even though I eat seeds and grain, I prefer to eat small bugs. I build my nest on the ground and weave a roof out of straw and grass to hide it from other birds and animals. Sometimes people think I am a Starling, but they're wrong! I'm just me, a beautiful Meadowlark.

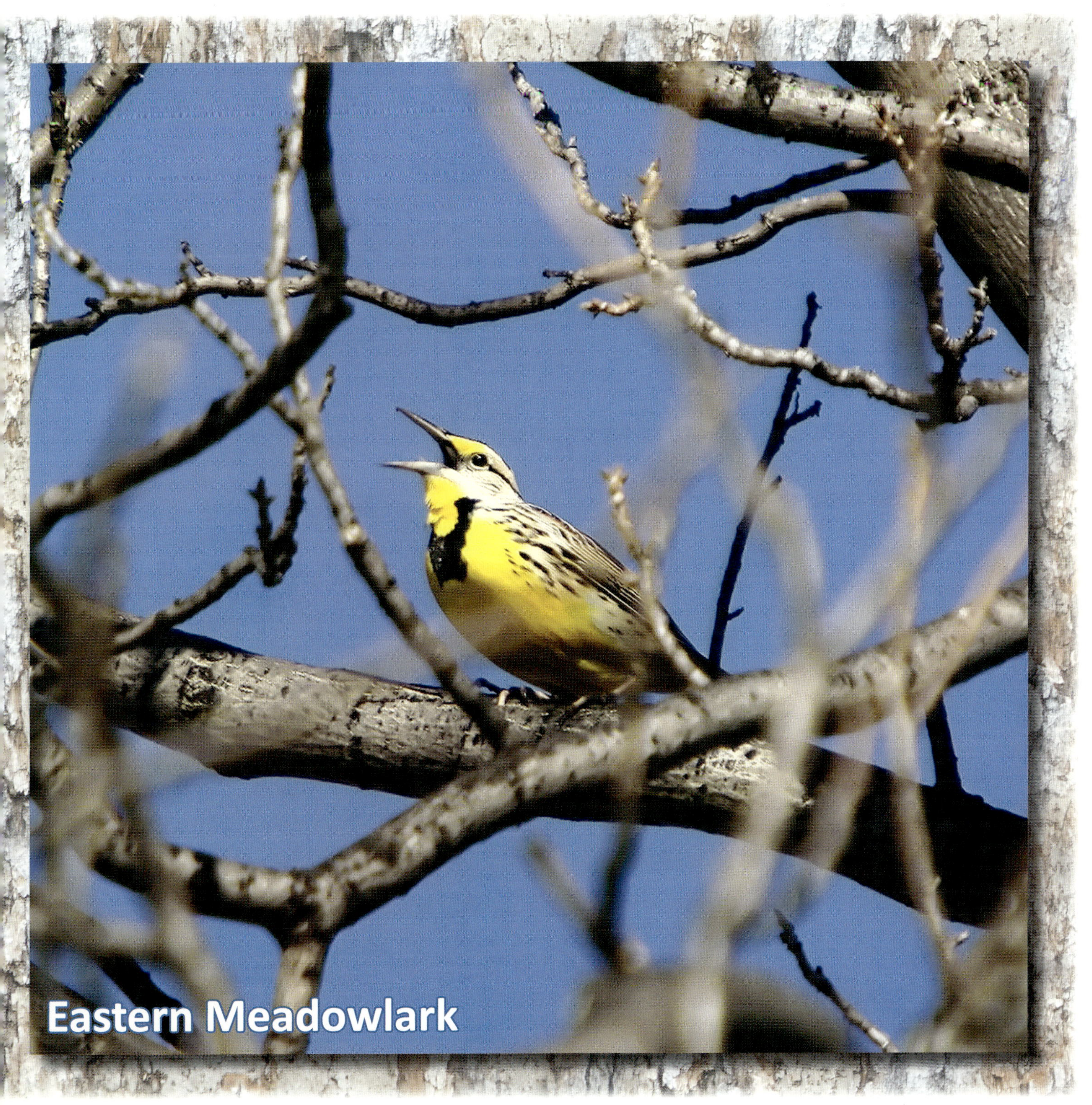

Eastern Meadowlark

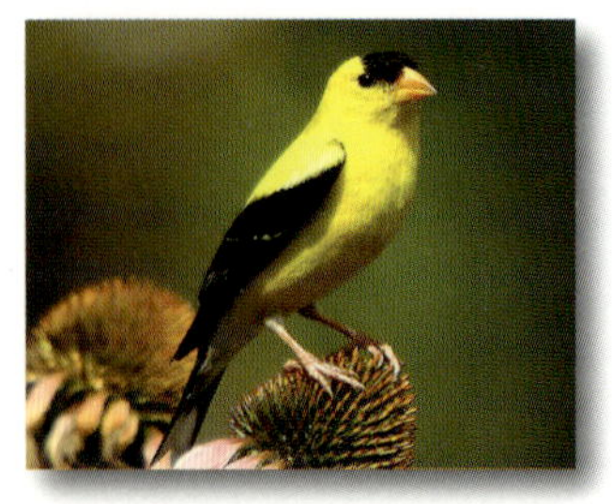

Goldfinch

I'm a male Goldfinch. You can tell because

of my bright yellow and black feathers.

If you have a bird feeder in your yard,

I might have my dinner at your house.

But I cannot stay long.

I have to hurry back to feed my babies.

That's the job of daddy Goldfinches.

We feed the babies while the mommy flies

off to lay more eggs. Just call me Mr. Mom!

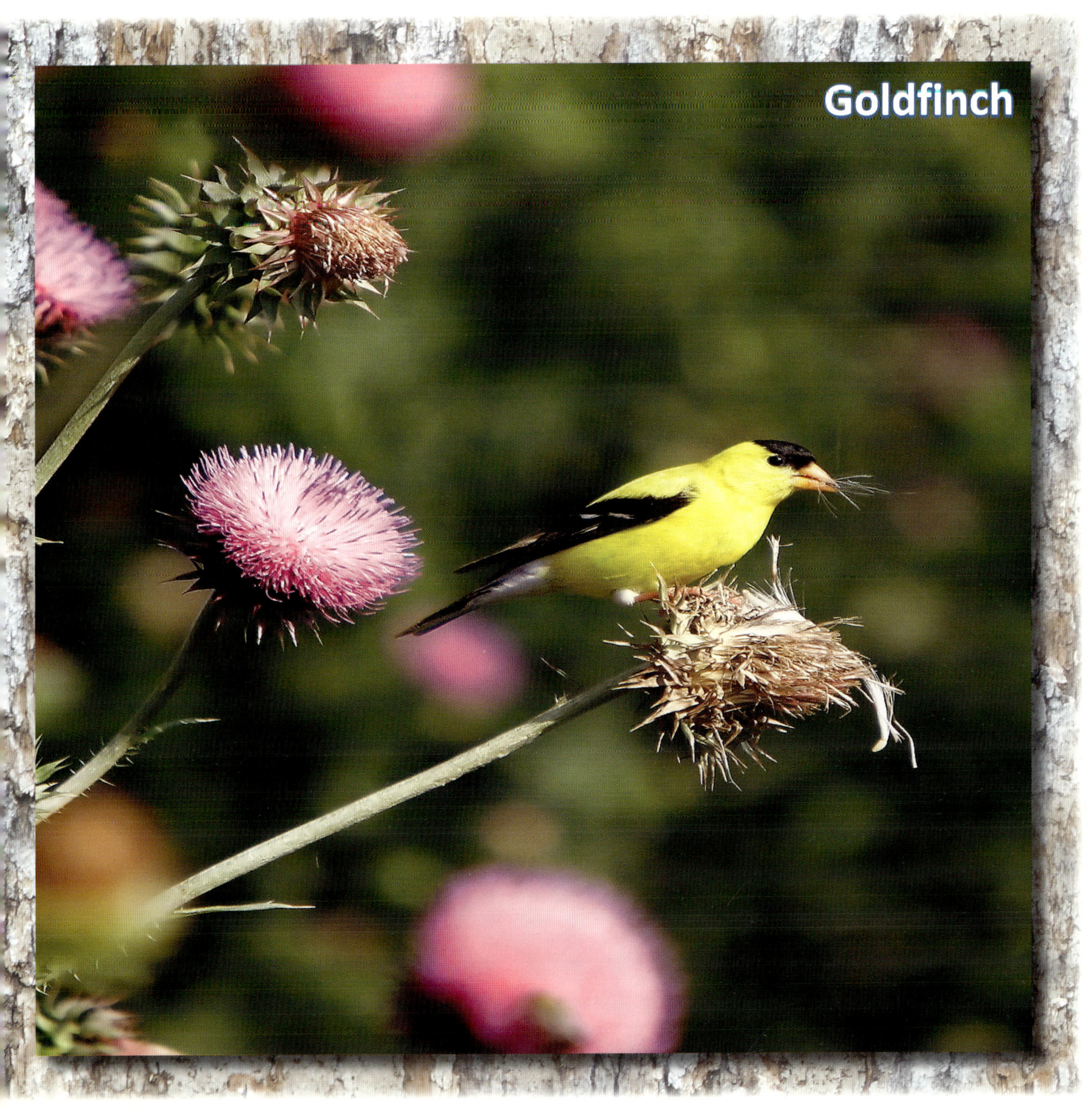
Goldfinch

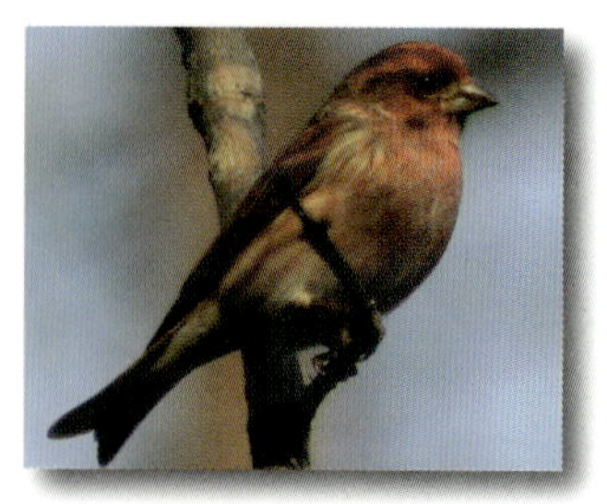

Purple Finch

No, you are not seeing things!

I'm really red; but, for some reason,

people call me a Purple Finch.

I love to eat seeds, flower buds, and fruit.

There are fewer Finches around now

because our cousins, the House Finches,

steal our nests, eat our food

and chase us away!

BOO ....!

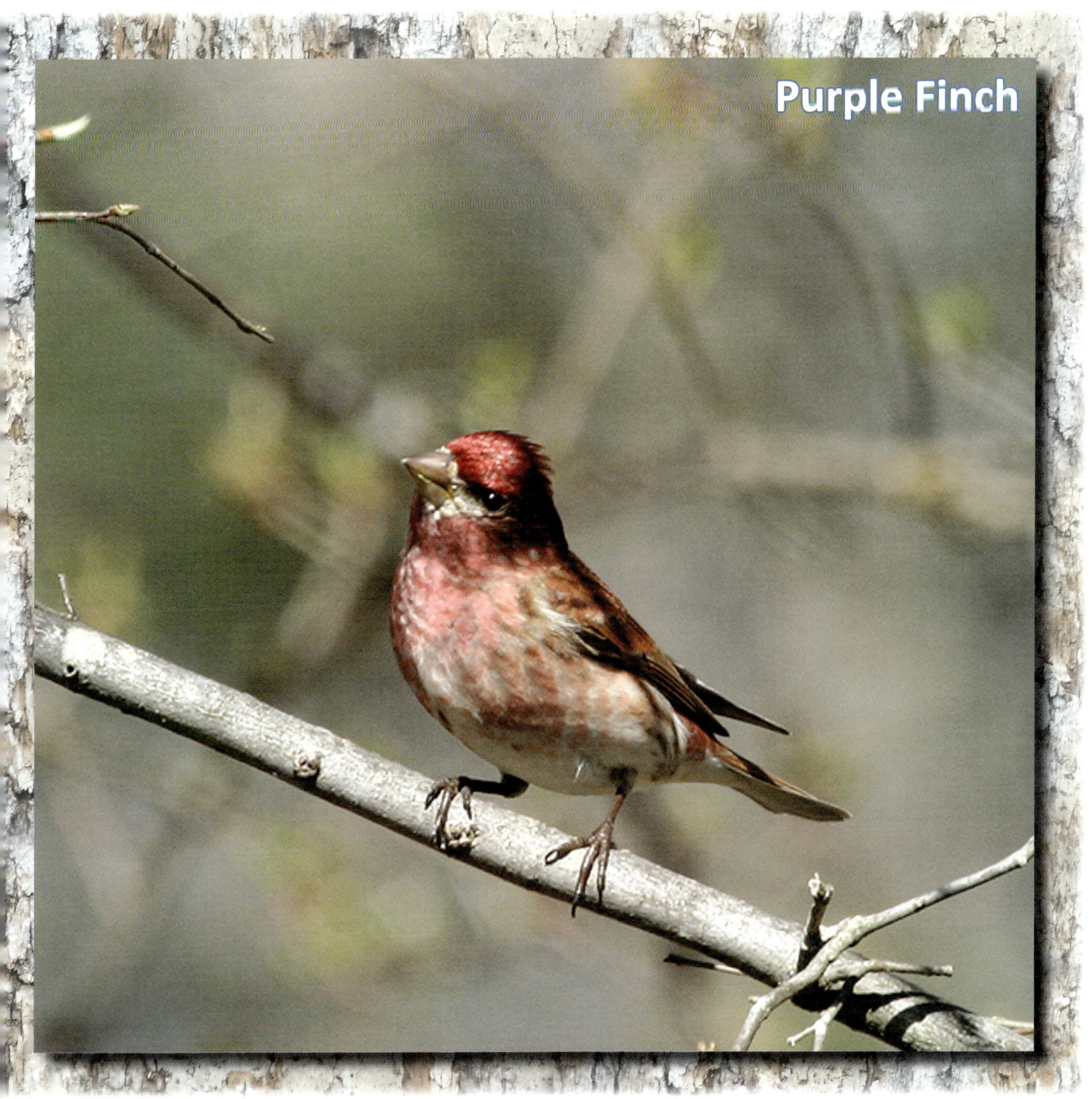
Purple Finch

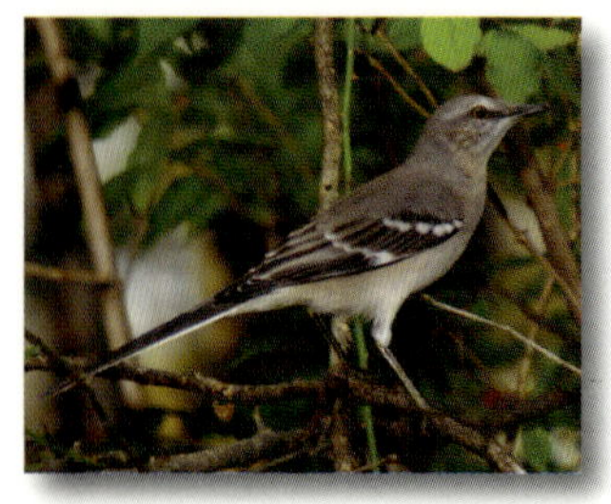

Mockingbird

Do you hear that bird calling?

I like that sound. Maybe I will try it.

Tweet, tweet, tweet.

I like it! I think I will copy it. Oh, there's another bird calling. I like that call, too.

Mockingbirds can sound like a lot of different birds. Maybe someday I'll find the one that is just right for me!

Until then, I will keep on trying.

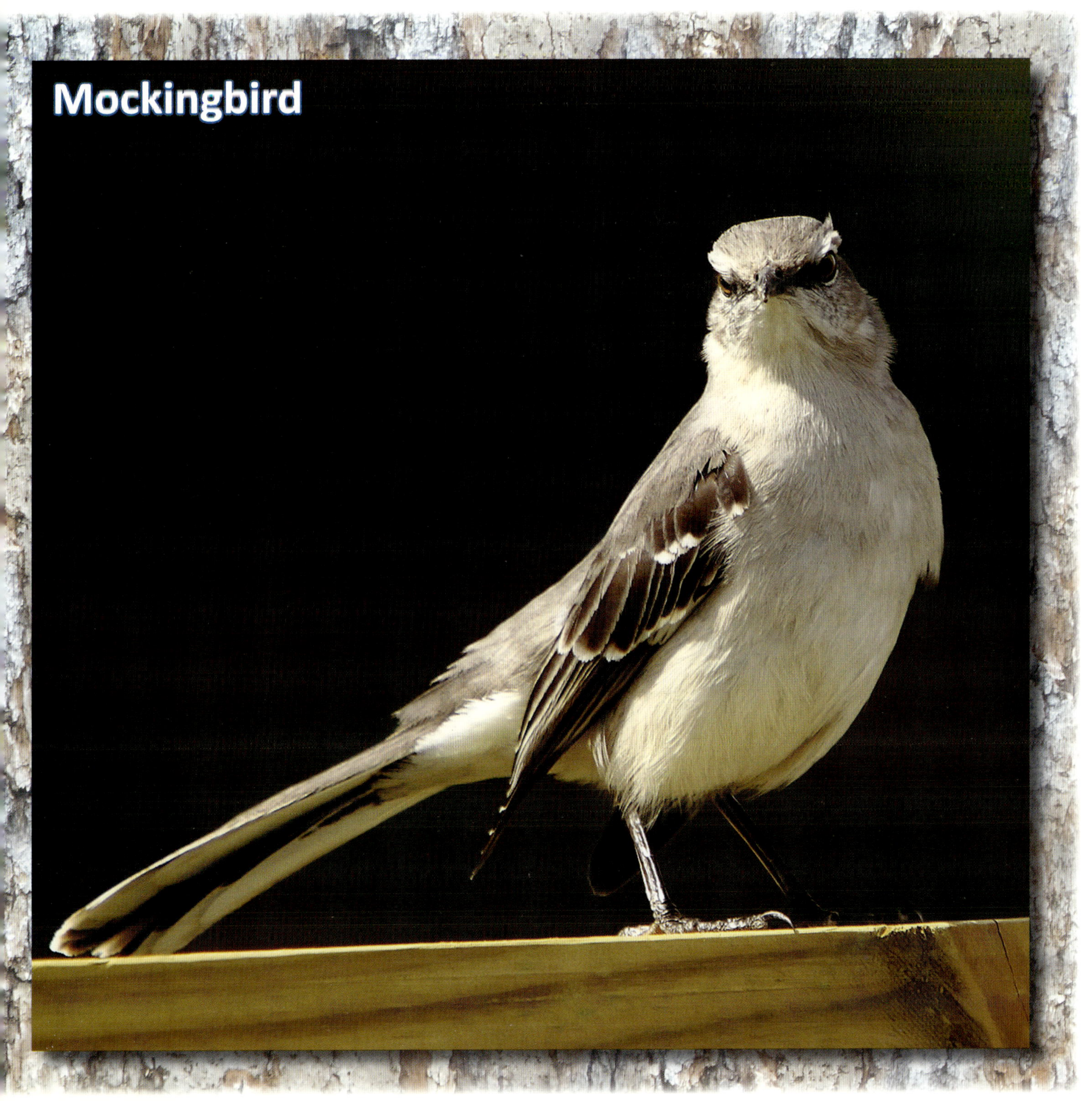
Mockingbird

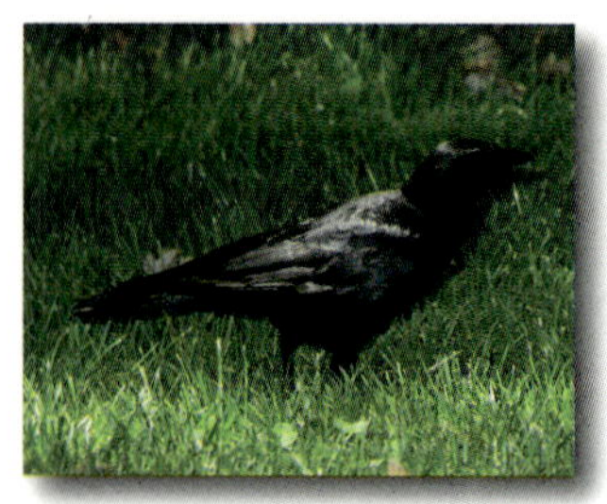

American Crow

Do you want to sound like me?
Awk, awk! Some people think I sing
a noisy song, but I think it sounds beautiful.
All my feathers are black, like ravens;
but I'm a little smaller. During the winter,
I like to sleep with my friends to keep warm.
Sometimes, thousands of crows gather
together. That's a lot of birds
and a lot of noise!

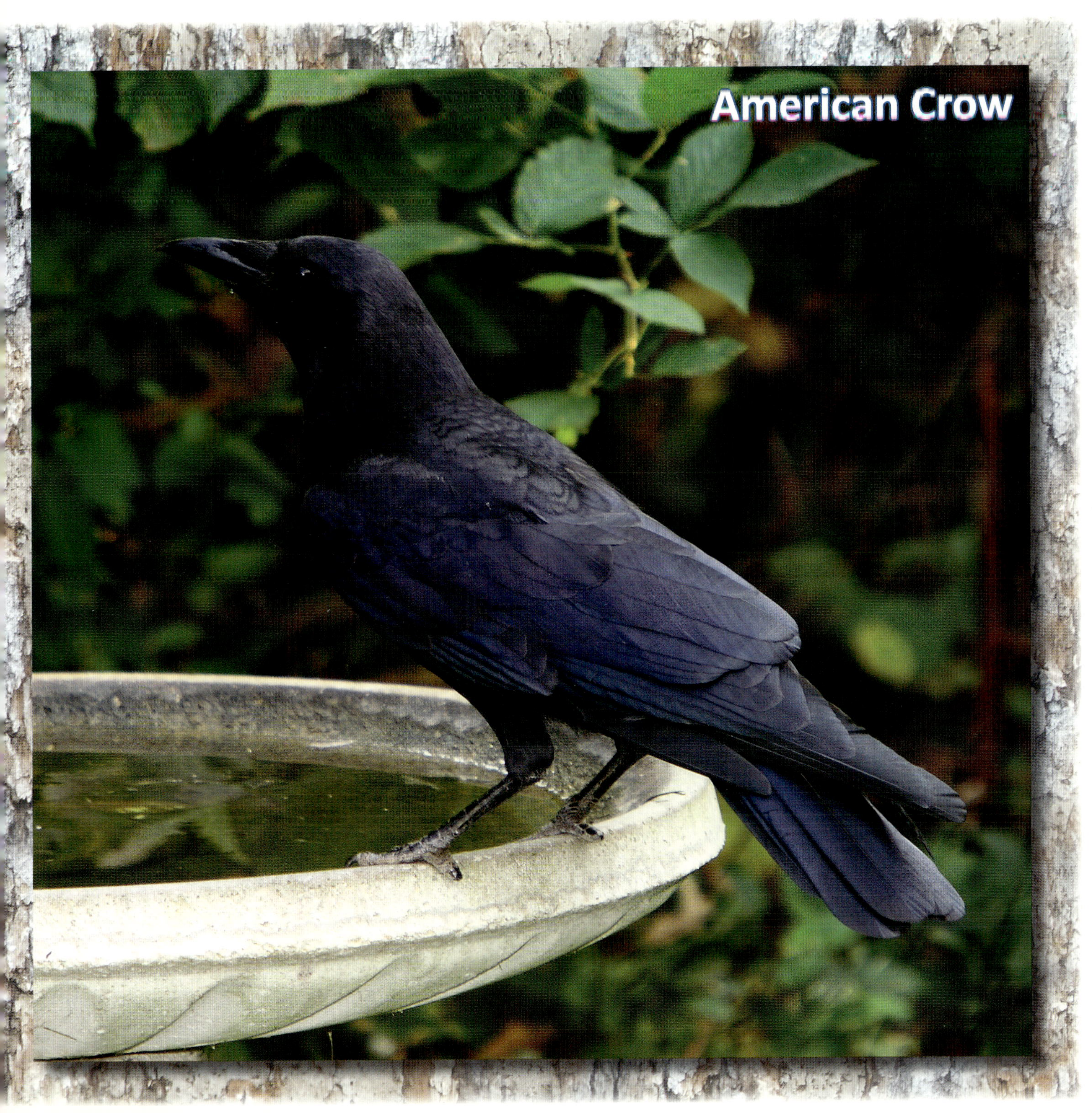
American Crow

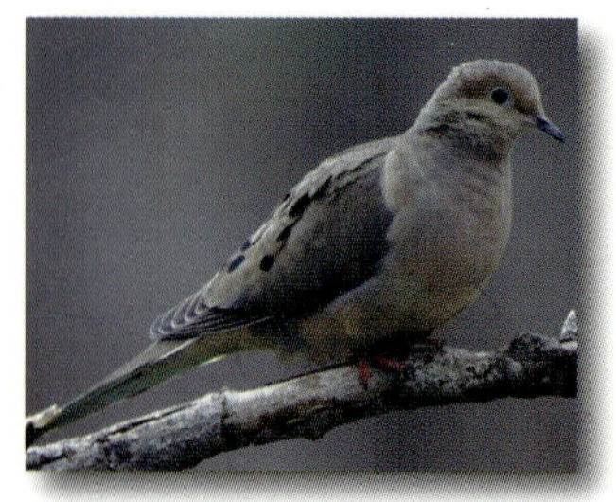

Mourning Dove

Have you heard me cooing?

I may sound sad; but, I'm really happy.

My name is Mourning Dove,

but some people call me a Turtledove.

I love eating all kinds of seeds.

I build a nest of twigs where

I lay my eggs. My babies are called *broods*.

I can raise several broods in one year.

That's a lot of babies to sleep in one nest!

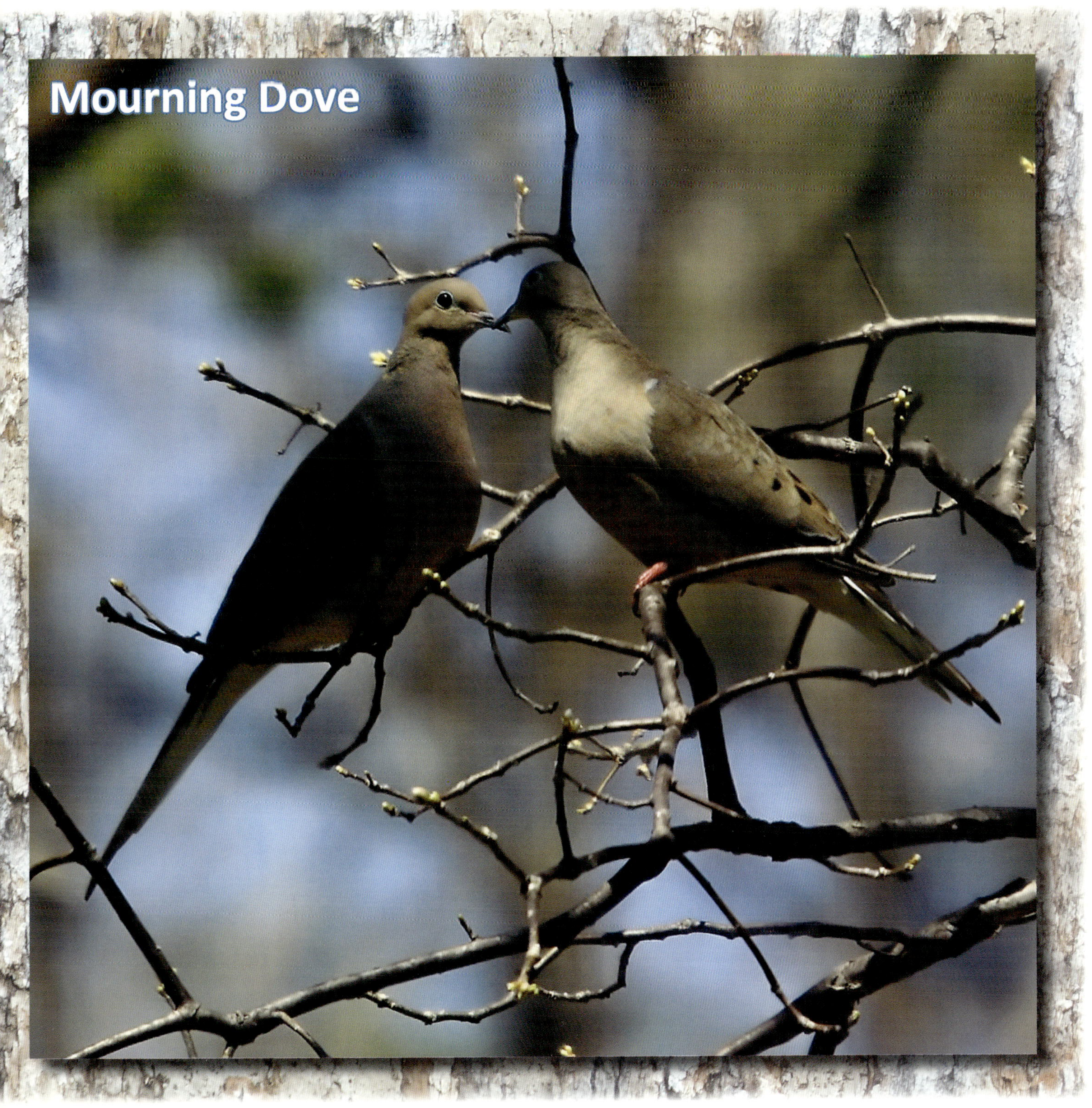
Mourning Dove

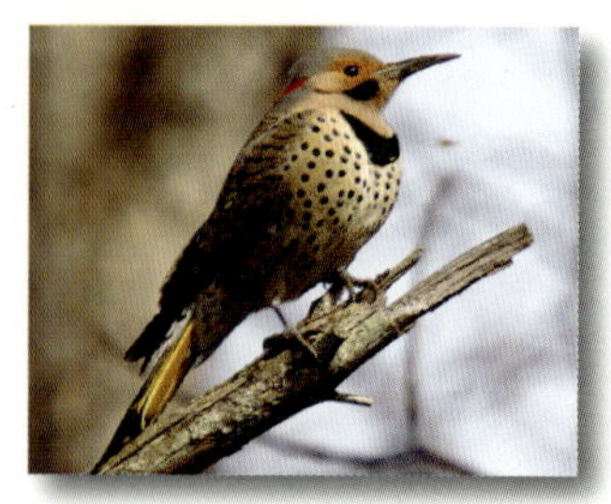

Northern Flicker

Do you think I'm pretty? I'm a Northern Flicker,

and I'm part of the Woodpecker family.

I like to eat fruit, berries, seeds and nuts.

I also eat insects that crawl on the ground,

like ants. If I'm quick, I can catch a bug

that is flying in the air, too!

My nickname is the "Yellowhammer,"

and I'm the state bird of Alabama.

Imagine that!

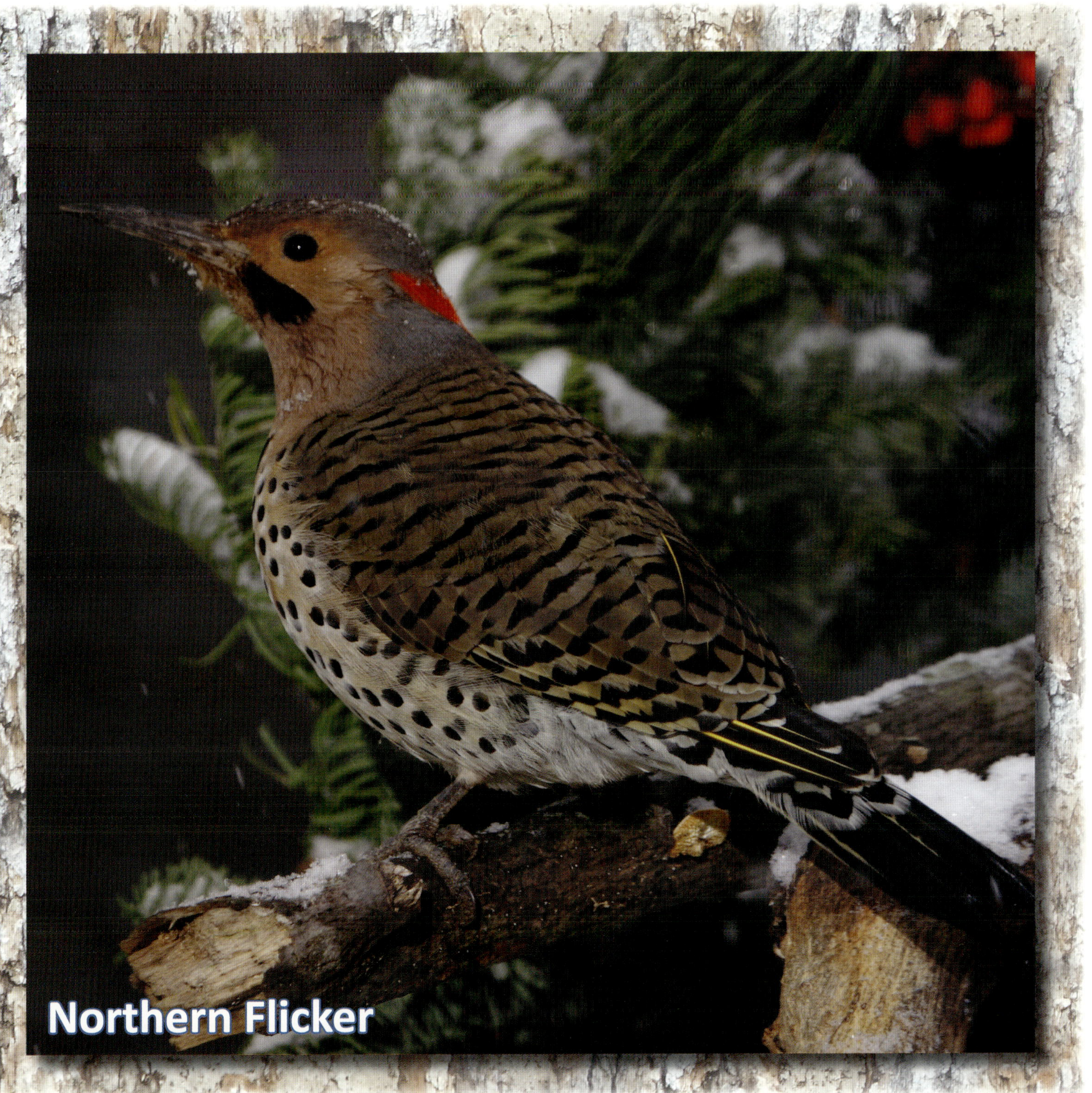
Northern Flicker

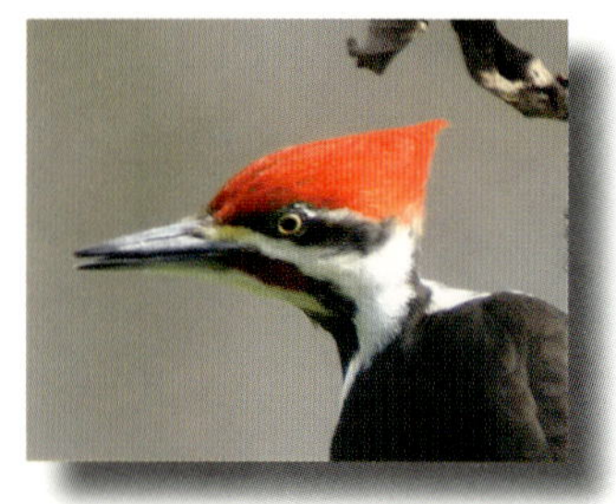

Pileated Woodpecker

Hi, there! I'm a Pileated Woodpecker.

Some people call me an "Indian Hen."

See my large, red head with a point at the back.

I am one of the biggest Woodpeckers in America.

I like to eat insects, especially beetle larvae and carpenter ants. When I make holes in trees to find food, sometimes I break smaller trees. Even though I am pretty, I can cause a lot of damage!

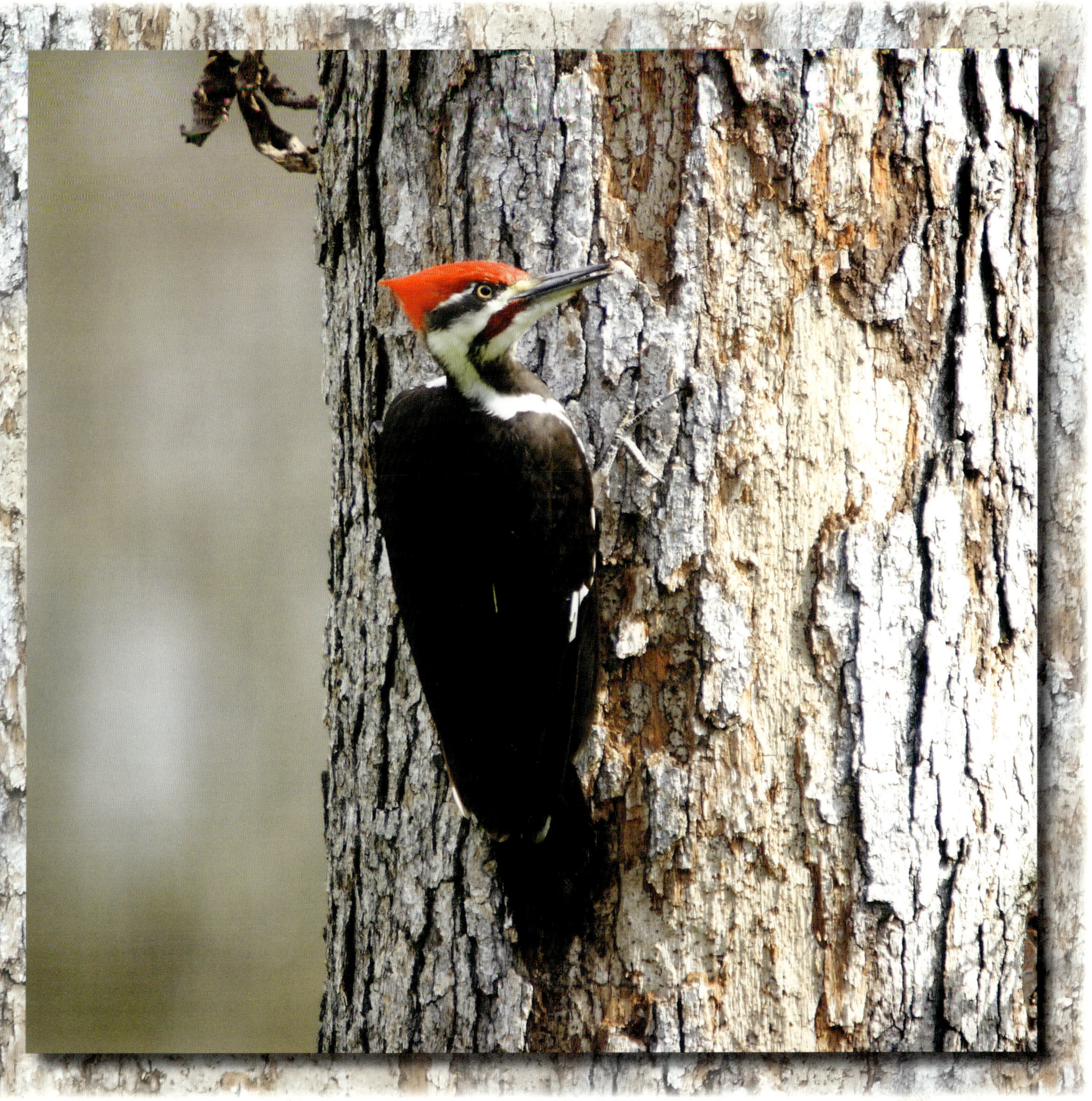

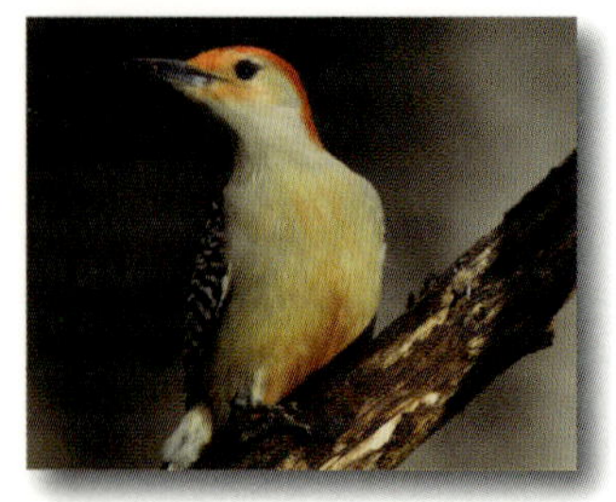

Red-bellied Woodpecker

I may not look like it,

but I'm a Red-bellied Woodpecker.

I use my pointed beak to poke holes in

tree trunks where I find bugs. When I make holes

in the trees, it sounds like "ratta-tat-tat".

If there are bugs living in the wood

in your house, I'll make holes there, too!

I need to get back to work ...

"ratta-tat-tat".

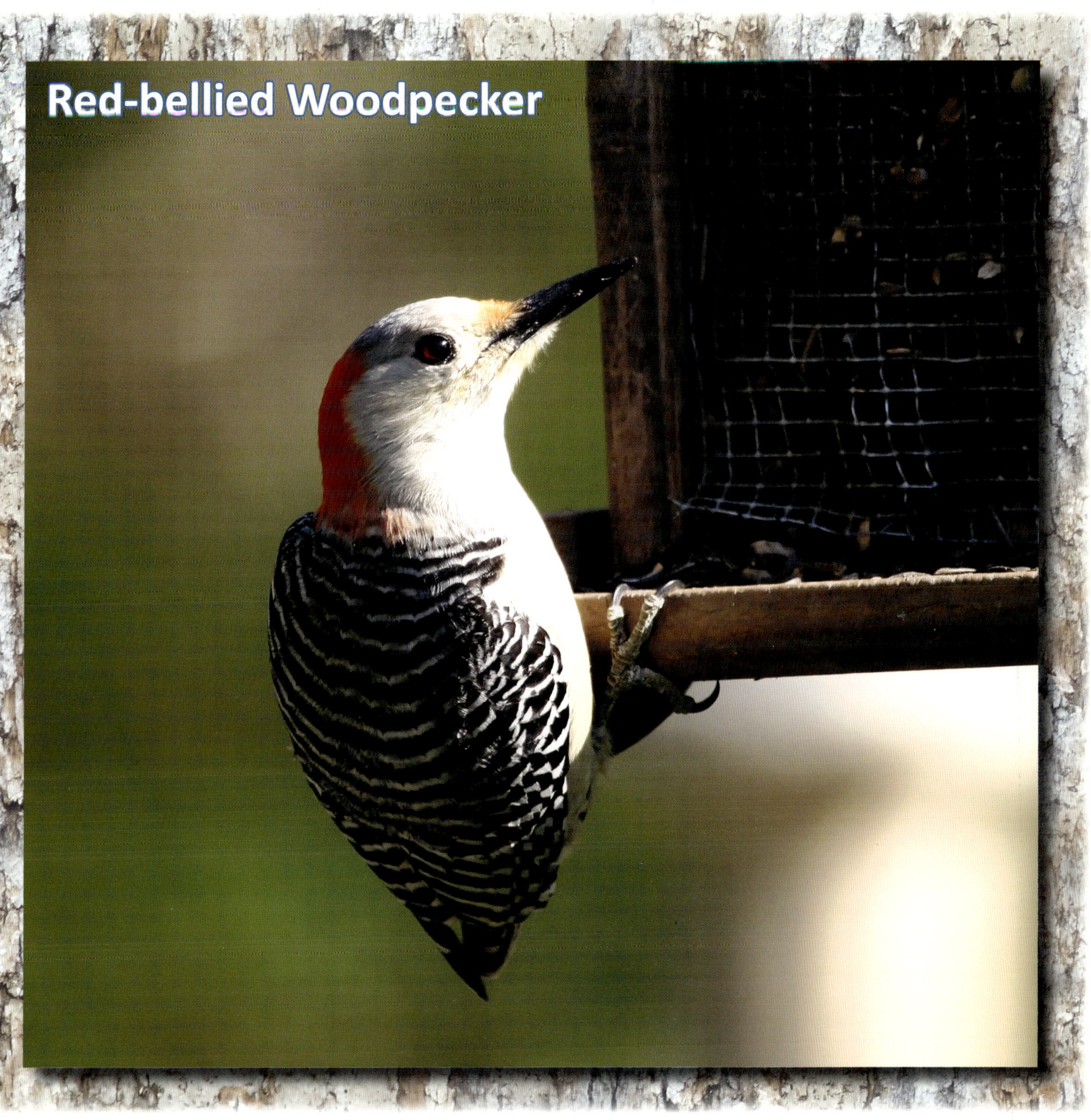
Red-bellied Woodpecker

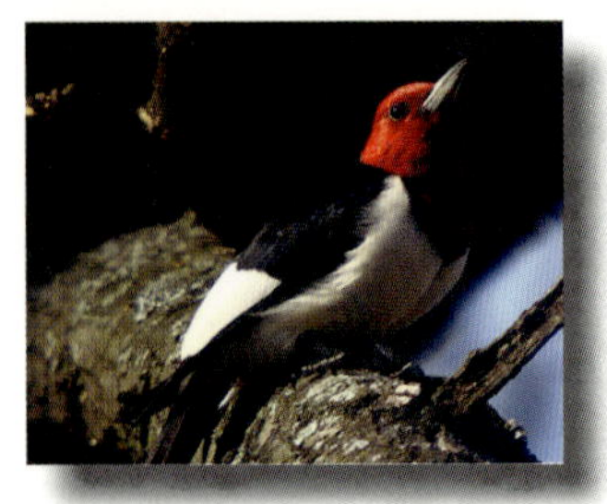

Red-headed Woodpecker

Don't you think I'm a beautiful bird?

People call me a Red-headed Woodpecker.

See my red head. It is smooth on top. I'm a bit different than other woodpeckers because I'm the only one who stores my food to eat later. Sometimes I take seeds, and even grasshoppers, and wedge them in tree bark. Then, when I get hungry, I just go get a snack from my favorite tree.

I think I'm pretty smart. Don't you agree?

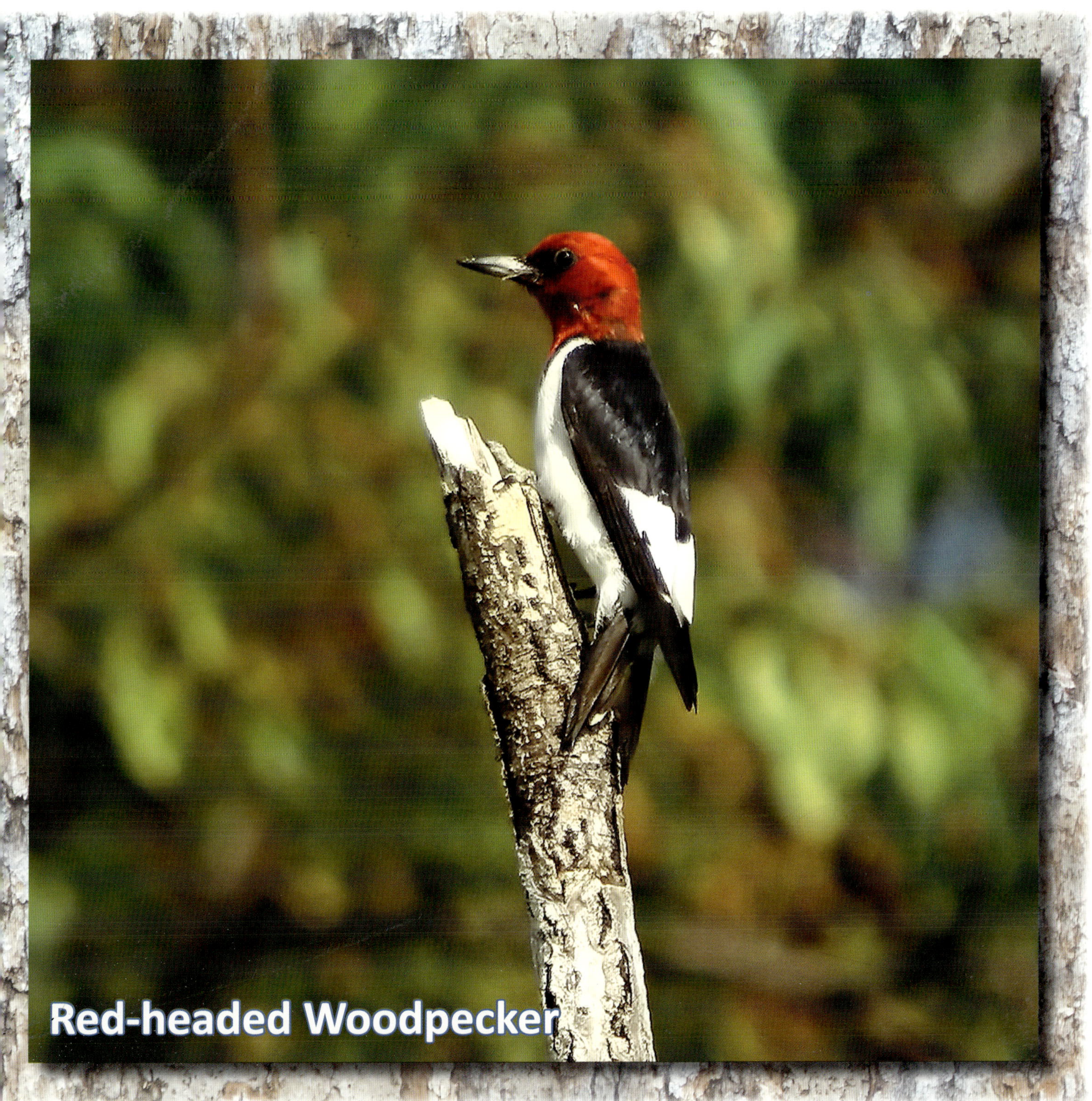

Red-headed Woodpecker

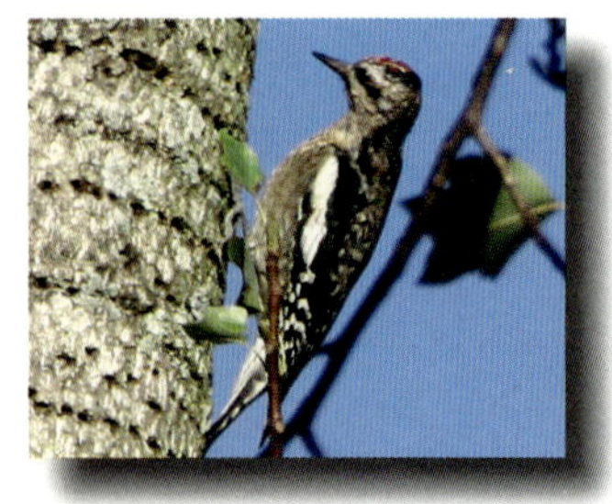

Yellow-bellied Sapsucker

I'm a Yellow-bellied Sapsucker, and
I am very important in the bird world because
I make little holes in trees to suck out the sap.
Then, other birds dig in my holes
to find their own food.
I'm not noisy like other woodpeckers.
Instead, I squeak, whine, or just keep quiet.
"Better seen than heard," is my motto.

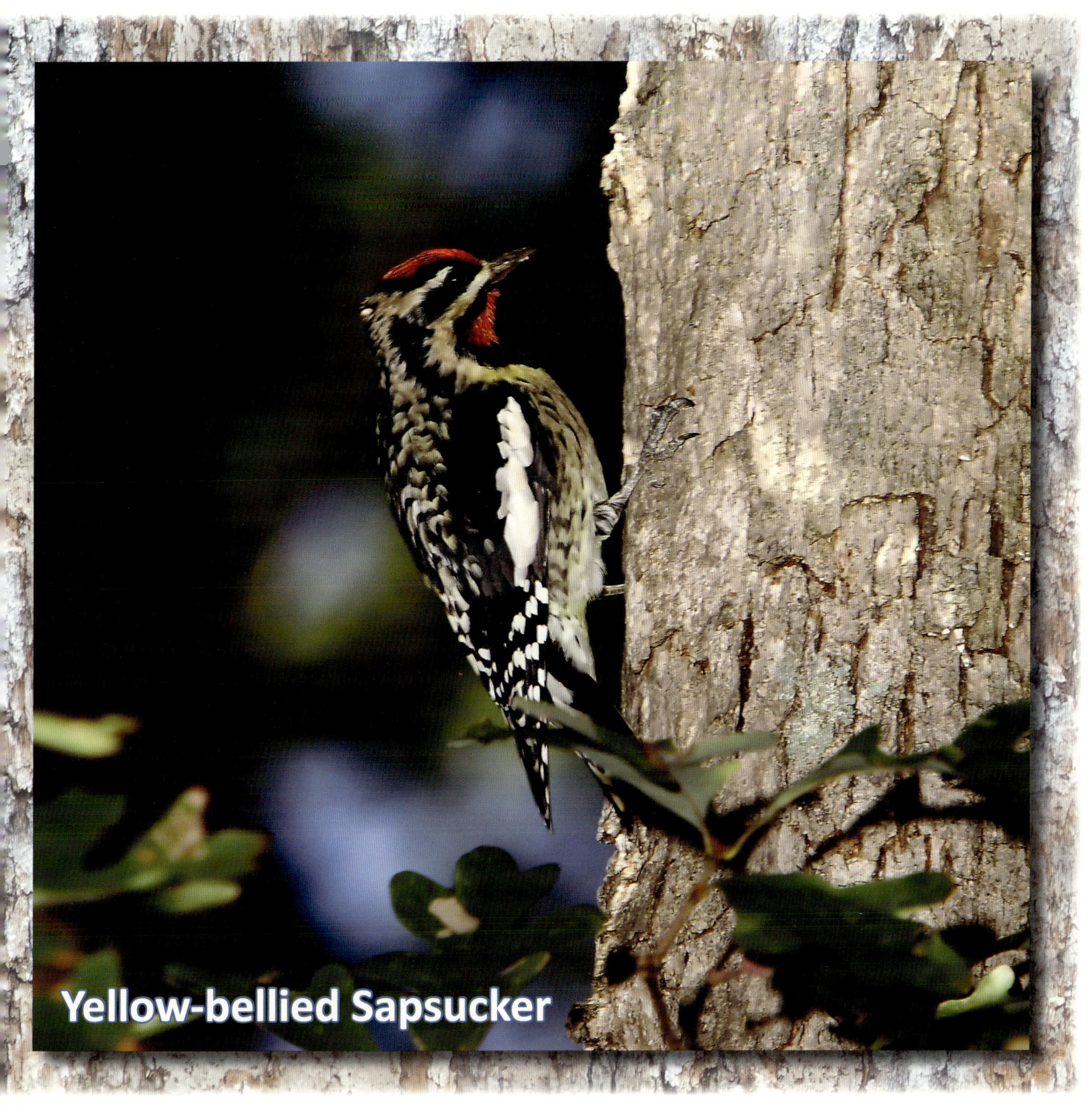
Yellow-bellied Sapsucker

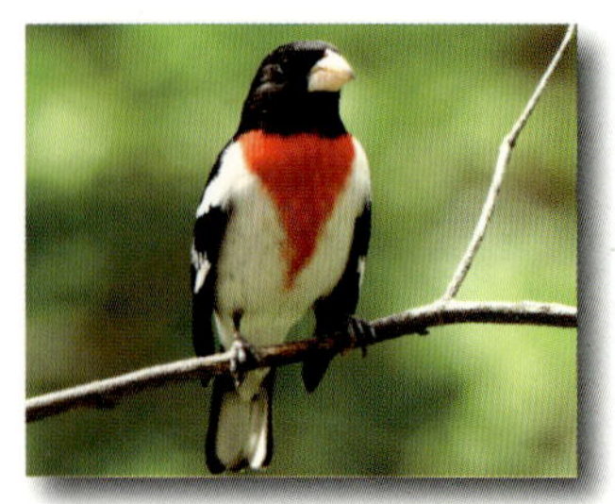

Rose-breasted Grosbeak

Grosbeaks are very colorful birds,

with red, black, and white feathers.

Our eggs are pale blue or green with brown spots.

When we sit on the eggs, we like to sing songs.

When our eggs hatch, our babies

only stay in the nest for 9 to 12 days.

Then they fly away.

They grow up so fast!

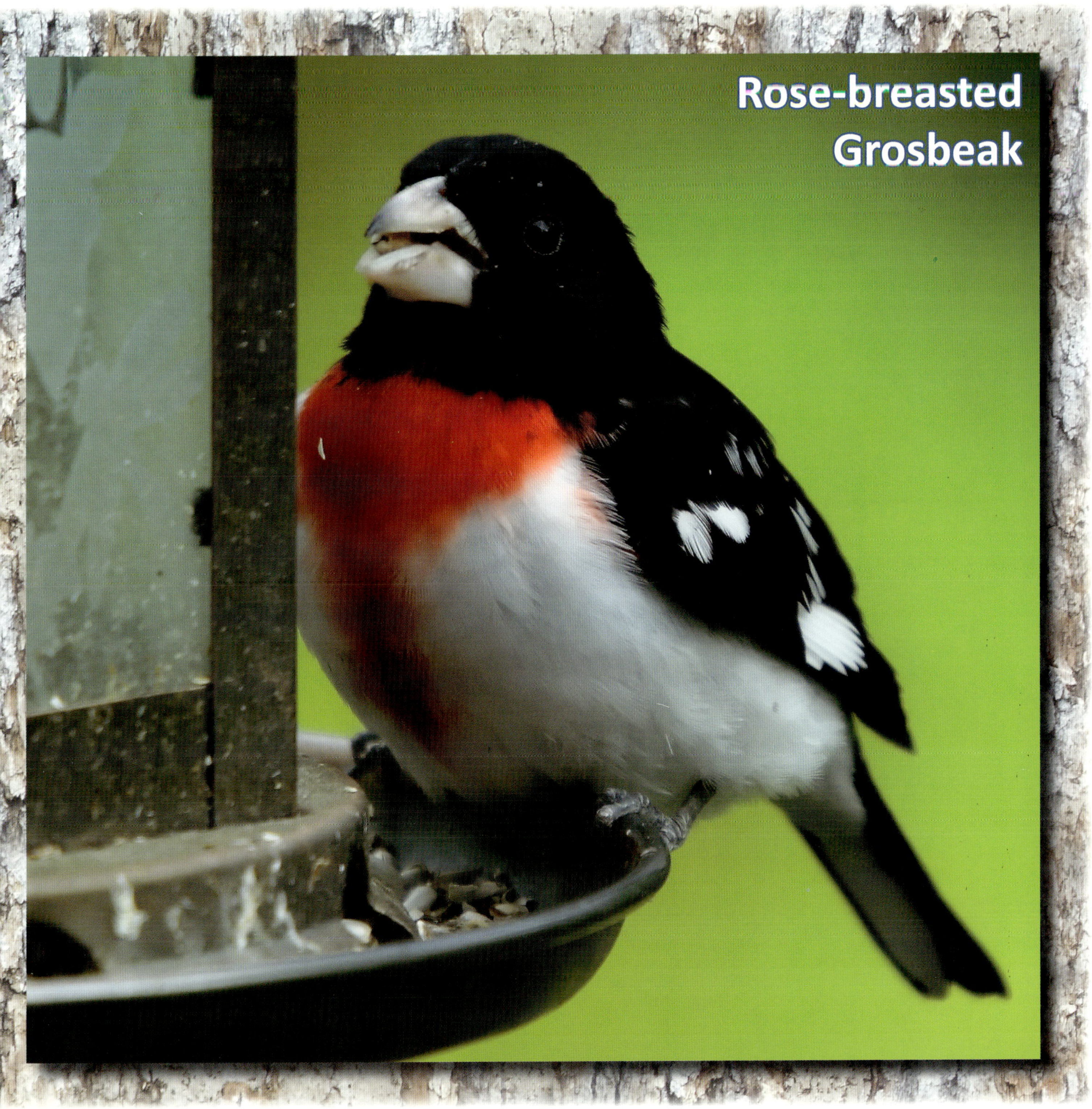
Rose-breasted
Grosbeak

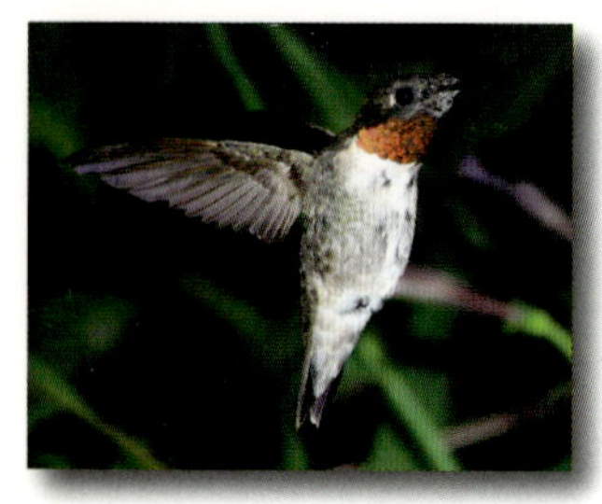

Hummingbird

Hummingbirds like me are very tiny.

We are the smallest birds in North America.

I'm so small that, if you see me,

you may think I'm a large bug.

When it's cold in the Piedmont,

I fly to Mexico to spend the winter.

It takes me 18 to 24 hours to fly

across the Gulf of Mexico.

But, I love that wonderful, warm sunshine!

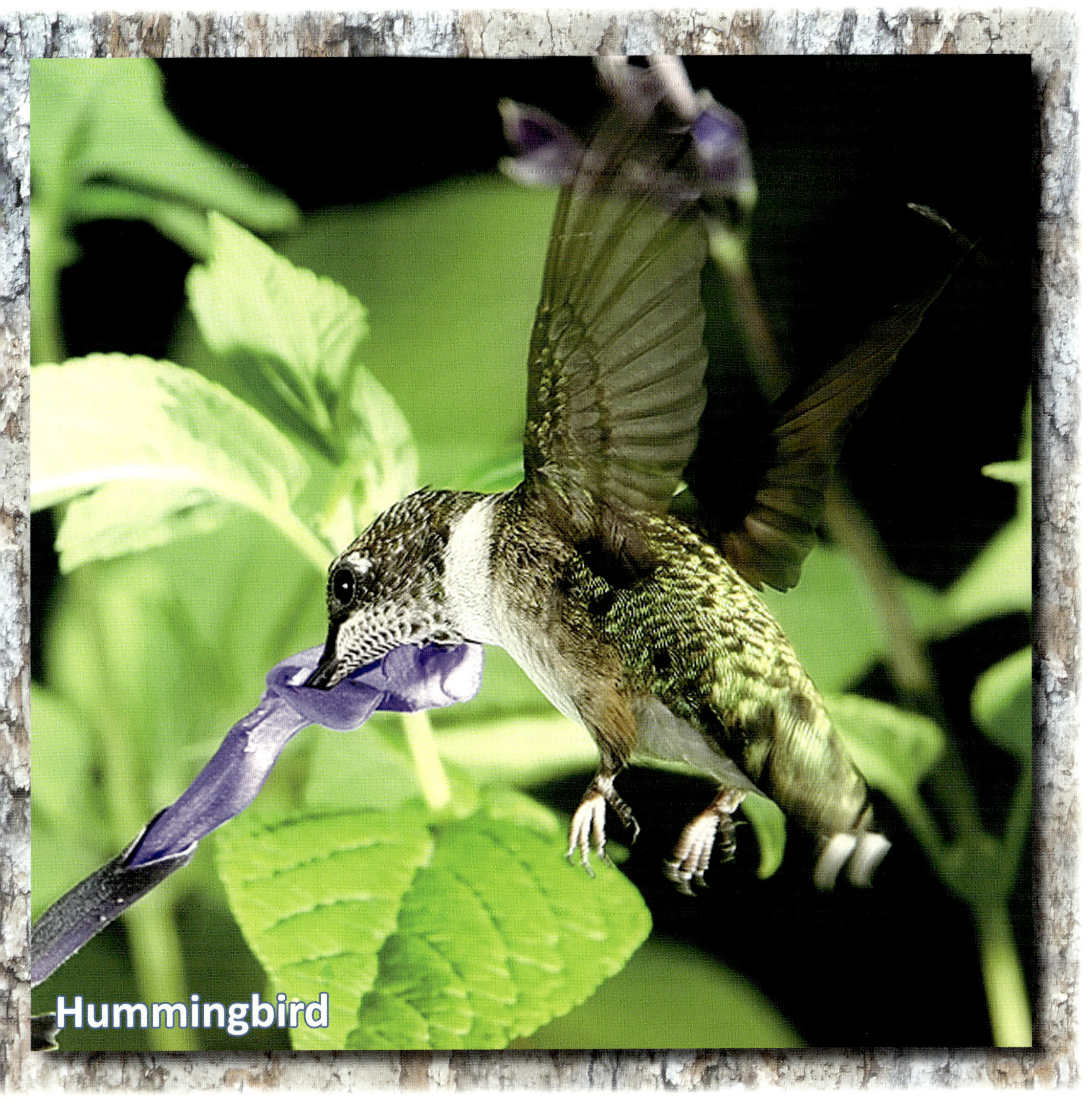

Hummingbird

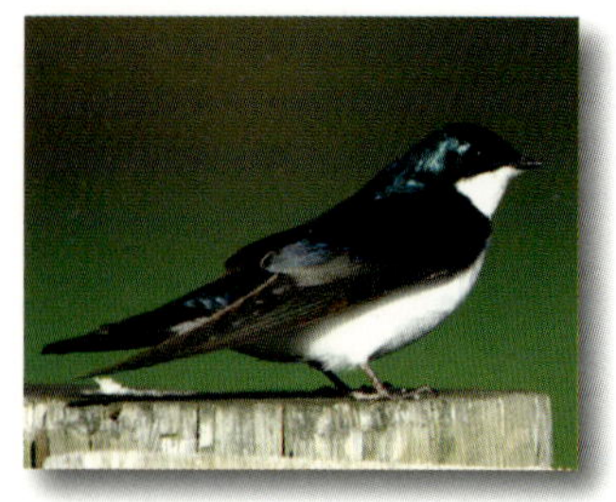

Tree Swallow

Tree Swallows live in wet places like streams and flooded meadows. Since we eat both plants and seeds, we stay in cold areas later than most birds. When we migrate to warmer places, we fly during the day in large groups called *flocks*. At night, we sleep in bird houses or in the trees. Sometimes I fly with thousands of my friends ... that's a big bird party!

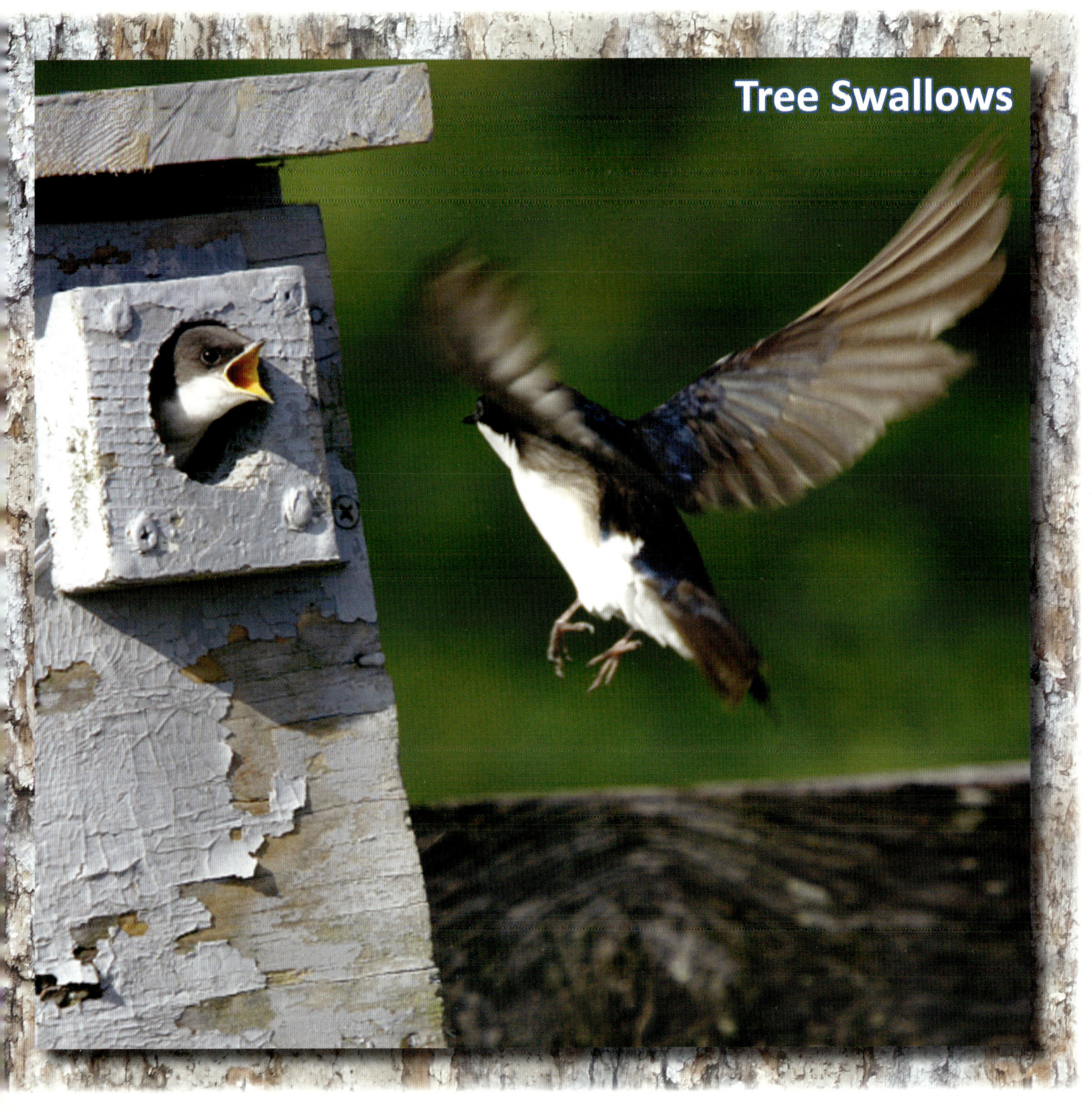
Tree Swallows

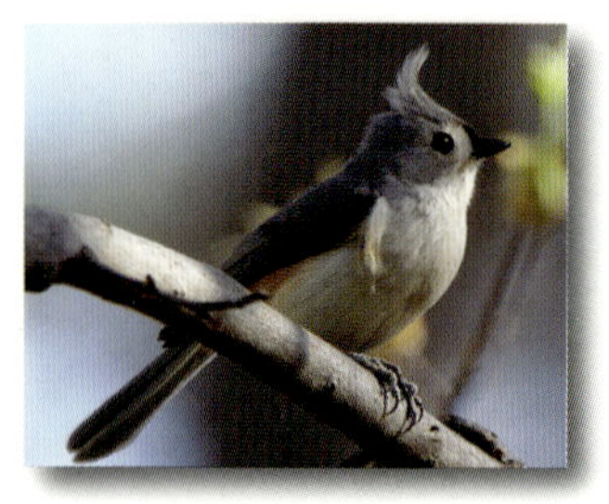

Tufted Titmouse

Have you seen me peeking in your window?

I'm a Titmouse, and I'm very curious!

Do you have some seeds for me?

I really like sunflower seeds and

I'm strong enough to fly away

with a whole peanut in my beak!

It may take me a while to open

the shell, but a delicious peanut

is worth working for, don't you think?

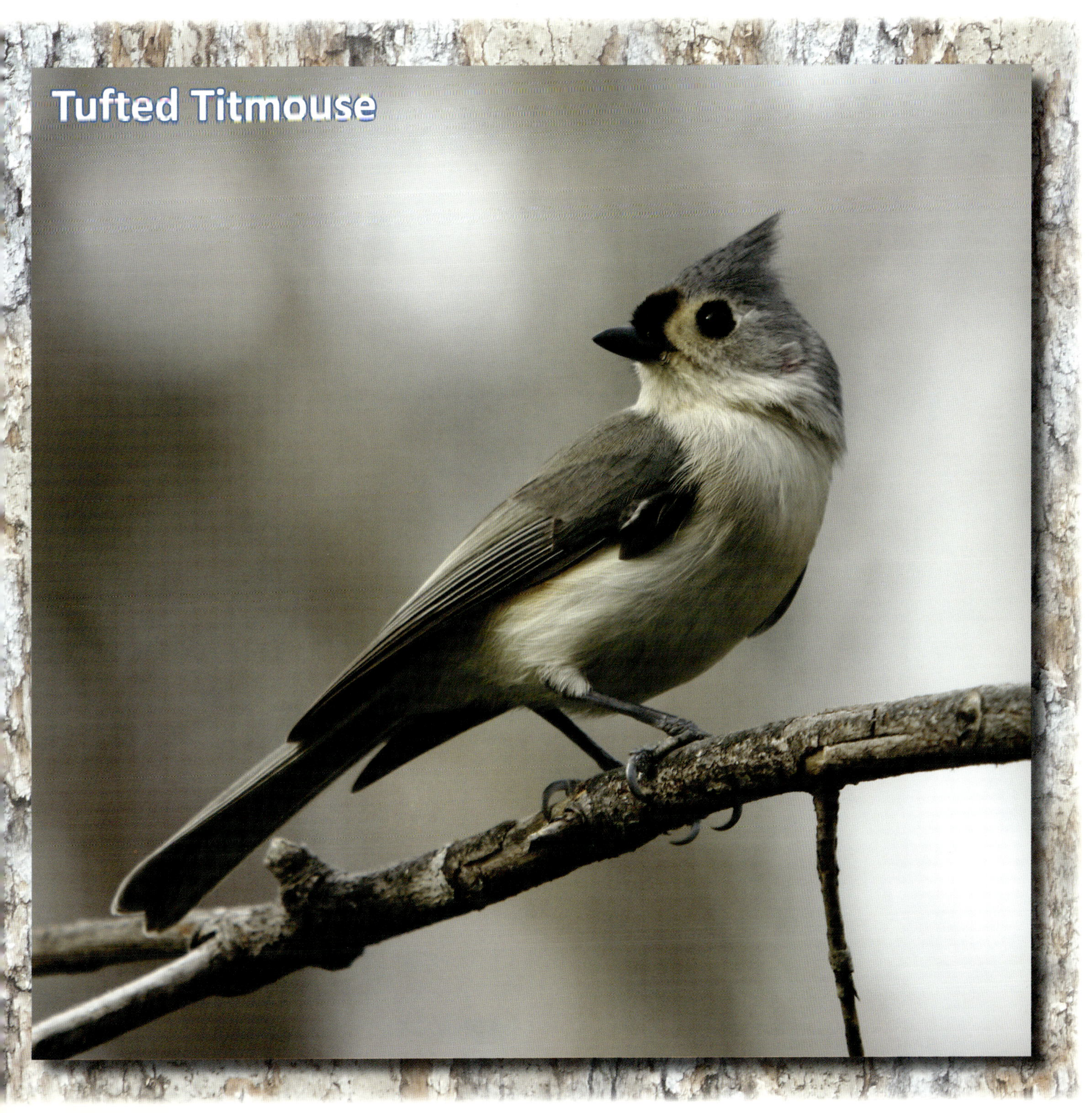
Tufted Titmouse

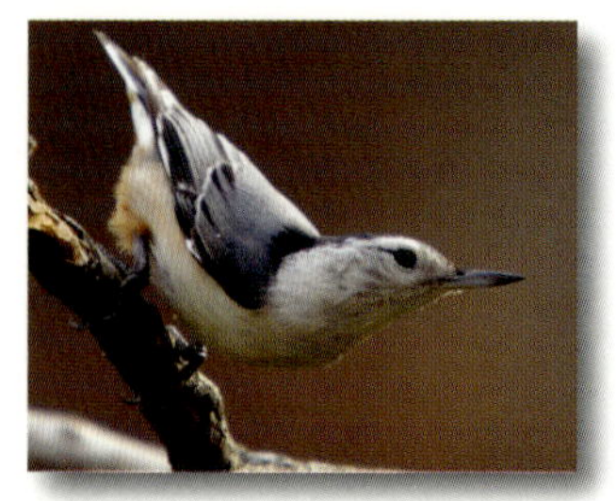

White-breasted Nuthatch

I'm a White-breasted Nuthatch.

See my pointed bill? I use it to wedge sunflower

seeds into cracks in the bark of trees.

Then I break open the shell to eat the meat.

You may be surprised to know that

I can climb trees upside down

to find the food other birds cannot see.

Most birds cannot do this.

I'm a very good food hunter!

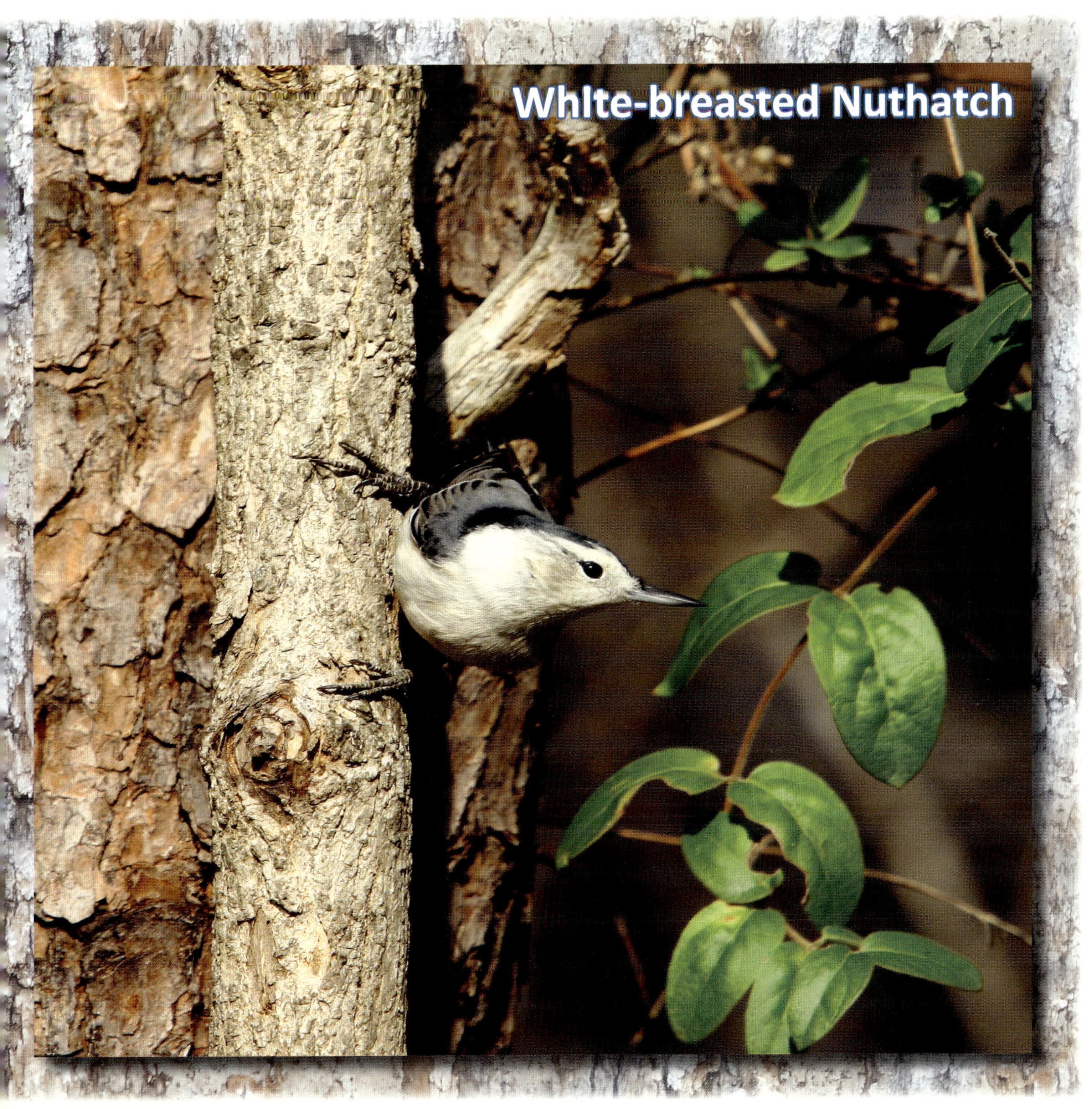
Whlte-breasted Nuthatch

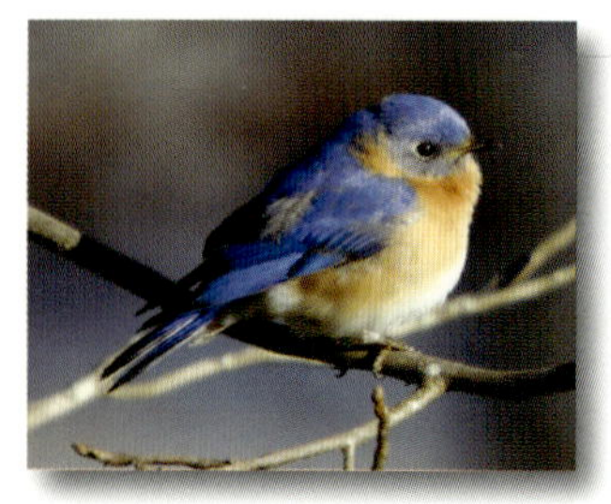

Eastern Bluebird

I'm an Eastern Bluebird. Once, there were many Bluebirds in the Piedmont; but soon other birds took our nests. People cleared land where we find insects and seeds to eat. Then there were not as many of us. Now, people have been working hard to help us build our homes again. Keep on helping us, and maybe we will come to your yard again soon.

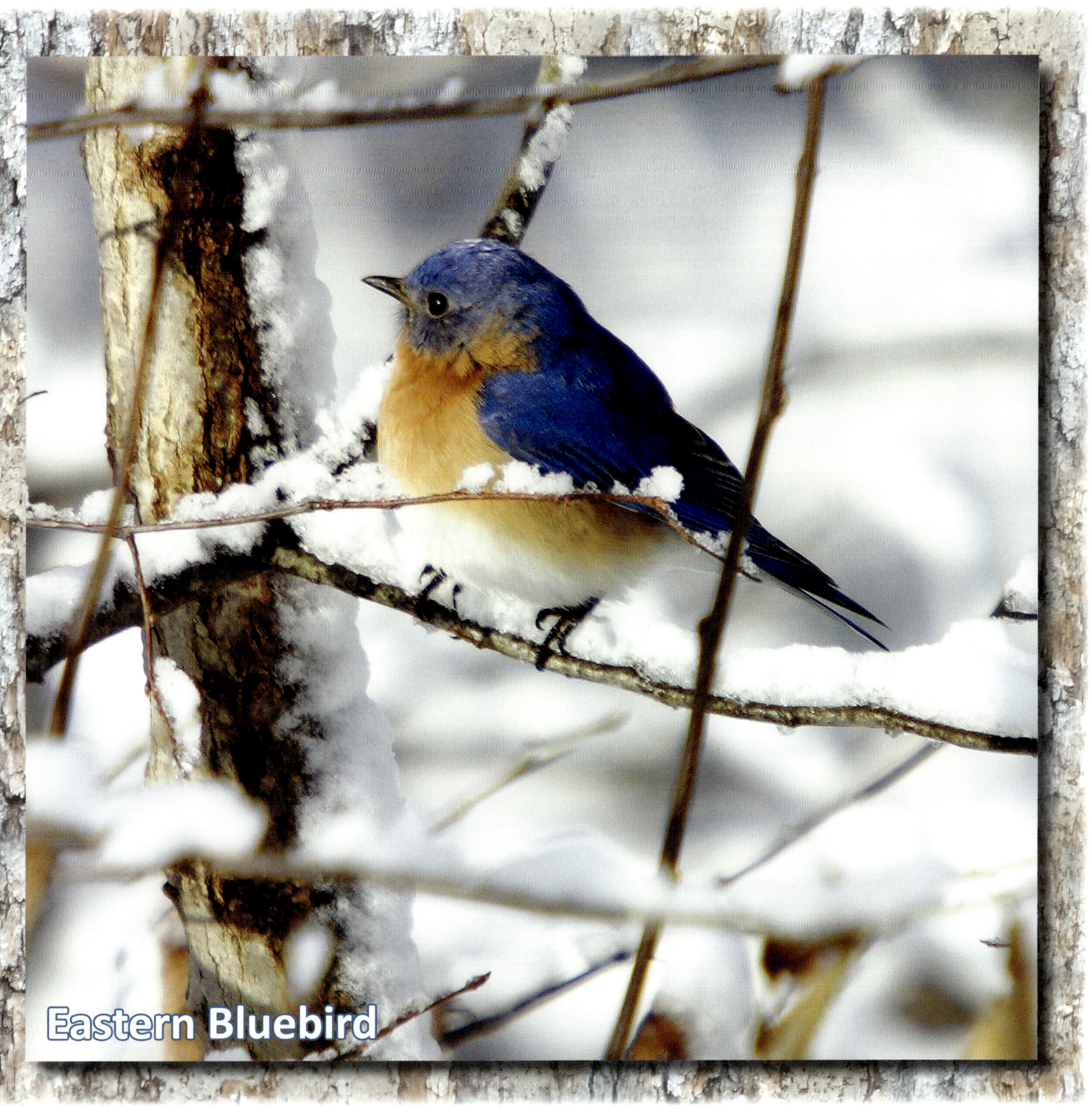

Eastern Bluebird

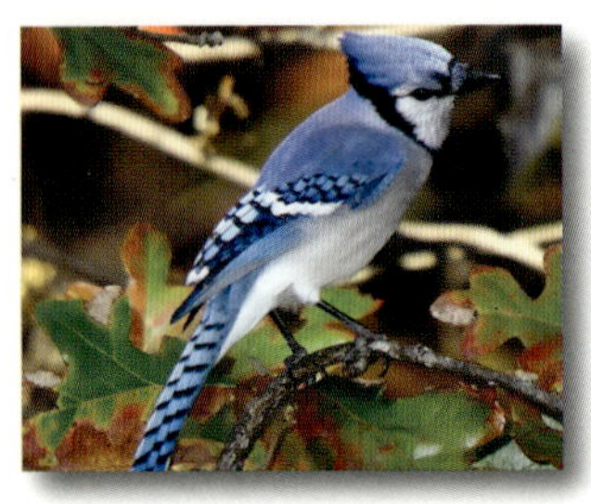

Blue Jay

I'm a Blue Jay and some birds say I'm a meanie.
I like to chase smaller birds from feeders
and eat the eggs in their nests.
If mean birds try to take my eggs,
I will chase them away by making loud,
screaming noises. I will chase you, too,
if you get too close to my nest!
Do you think I'm a meanie, too?
If you do, boo on you!

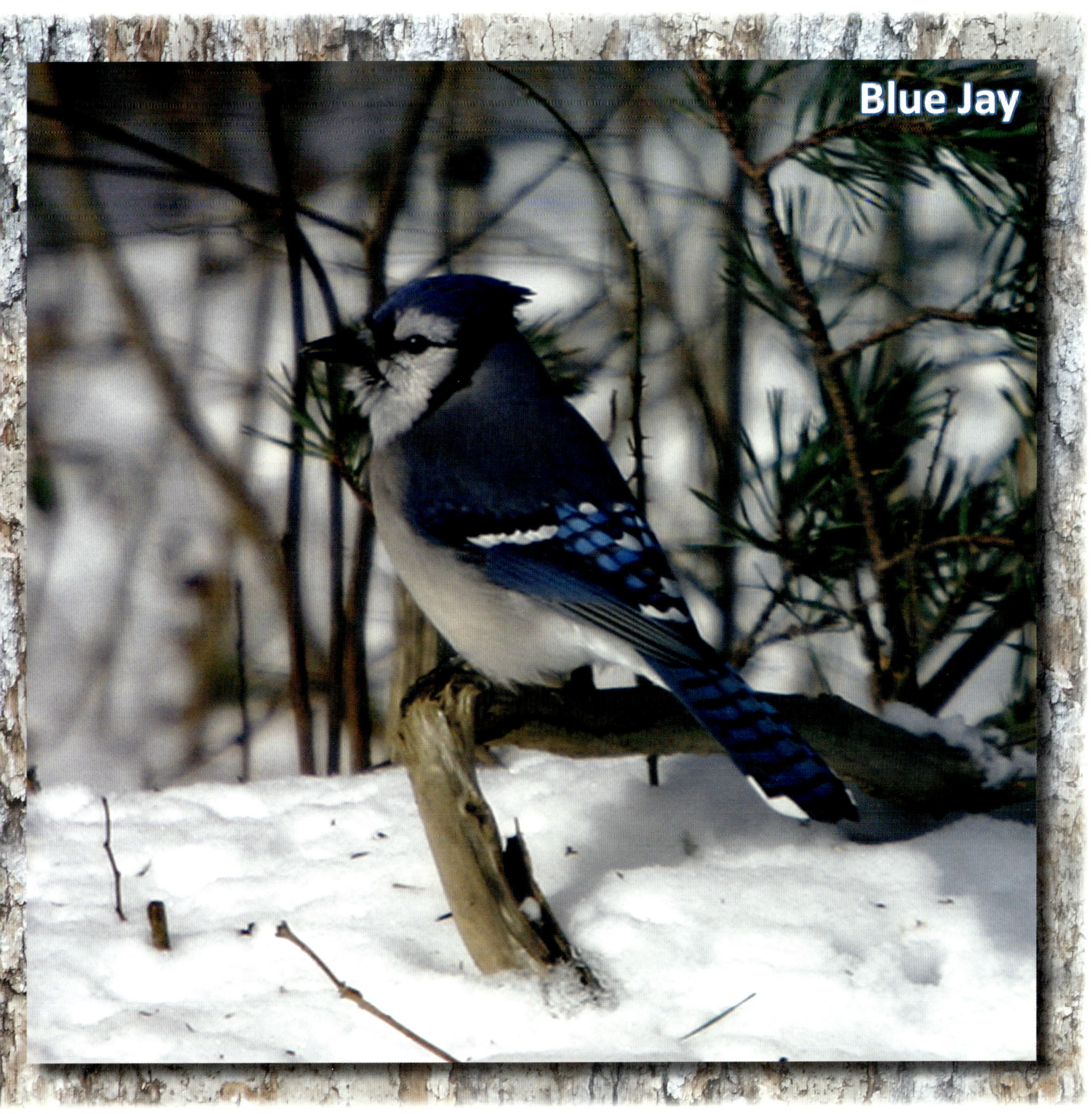
Blue Jay

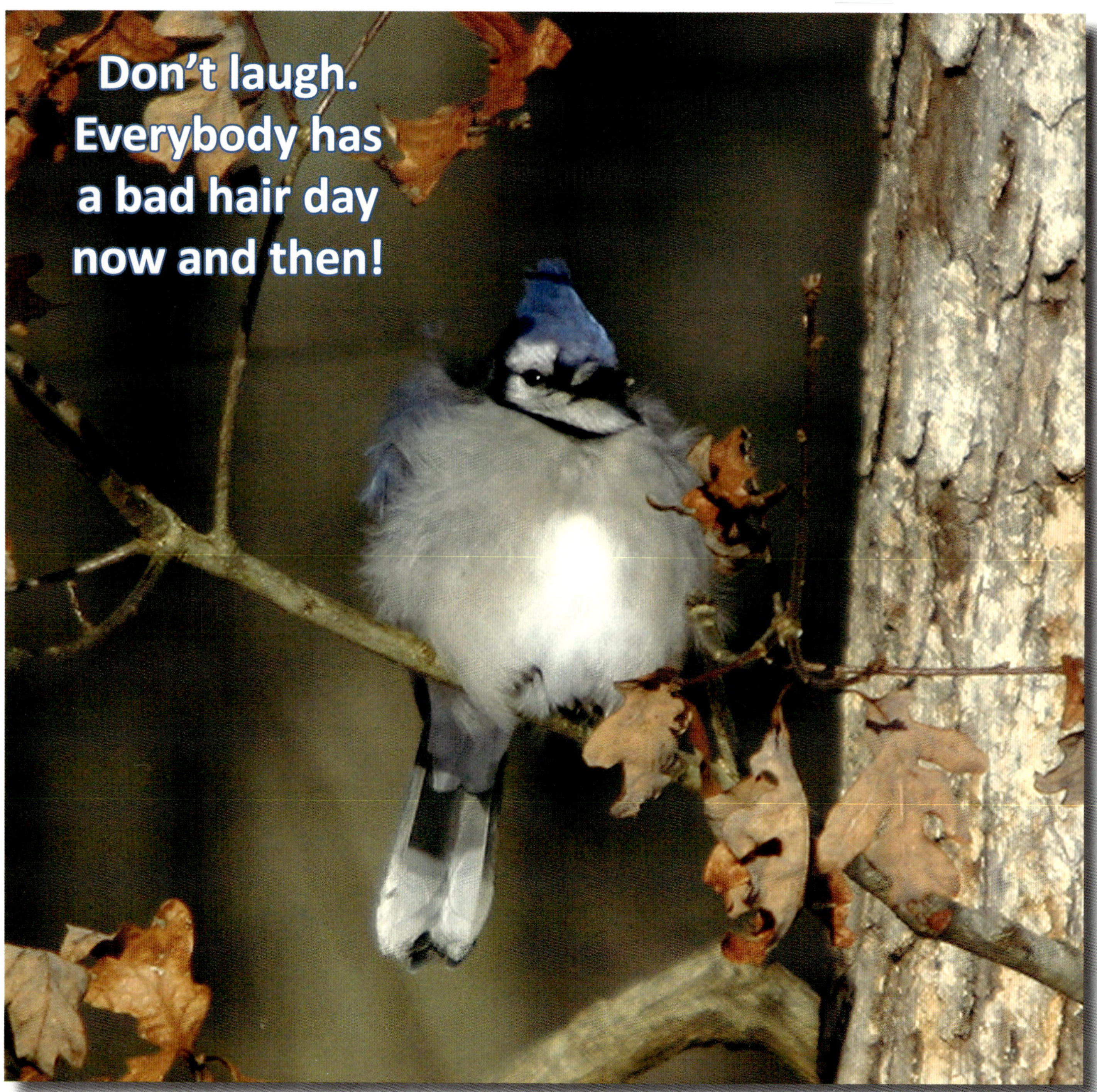
Don't laugh.
Everybody has
a bad hair day
now and then!